Essential Photoshop Basics

Kevin Wilson

www.elluminetpress.com

Essential Photoshop Basics

Publisher: Elluminet Press
Director: Kevin Wilson
Lead Editor: Steven Ashmore
Technical Reviewer: Mike Taylor, Robert Ashcroft
Copy Editors: Joanne Taylor, James Marsh
Proof Reader: Steven Ashmore
Indexer: James Marsh
Cover Designer: Kevin Wilson

eBook versions and licenses are also available for most titles. Any source code or other supplementary materials referenced by the author in this text is available to readers at

`www.elluminetpress.com/resources`

For detailed information about how to locate your book's source code, go to

`www.elluminetpress.com/resources`

Table of Contents

About the Author

Kevin Wilson has made a career out of technology and teaching others how to use it. After earning a master's degree in computer science, software engineering, and multimedia systems, Kevin worked as a tutor and college instructor, helping students master such subjects as multimedia, computer literacy and information technology.

He currently serves as Elluminet Press Publishing's senior writer and director, he periodically teaches computing at college in South Africa and serves as an IT trainer in England. His books have become a valuable resource among the students in England, South Africa and our partners in the United States.

Kevin's motto is clear: "If you can't explain something simply, you haven't understood it well enough." To that end, he has created the Computer Essentials series, in which he breaks down complex technological subjects into smaller, easy-to-follow steps that students and ordinary computer users can put into practice.

Acknowledgements

Thanks to all the staff at Luminescent Media & Elluminet Press for their passion, dedication and hard work in the preparation and production of this book.

To all my friends and family for their continued support and encouragement in all my writing projects.

To all my colleagues, students and testers who took the time to test procedures and offer feedback on the book

Finally thanks to you the reader for choosing this book. I hope it helps you to use your computer with greater ease.

1

Getting Started with Photoshop

To make full use of Photoshop CC you'll need a subscription to Adobe Creative Cloud. You'll then be able to download Photoshop CC and install it on your computer.

Creative Cloud subscriptions can be quite pricey but you can get a Photography Package for about £10 per month which includes Photoshop CC.

Downloading Photoshop

You can download Photoshop from Adobe's website. Adobe apps can be quite expensive, however you can take out a photographer's plan and use Photoshop for £10 a month. Open your web browser and navigate to...

`www.adobe.com/creativecloud`

Scroll down and click 'buy now' under the 'photographers' plan.

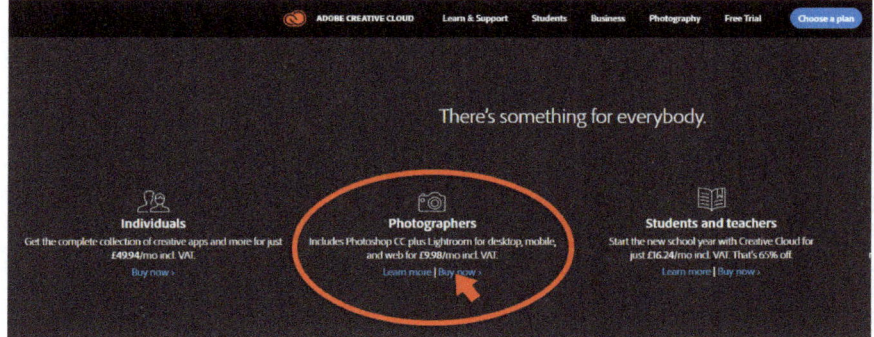

Enter your email address to use for your Adobe ID then click 'continue' to run through the buying process.

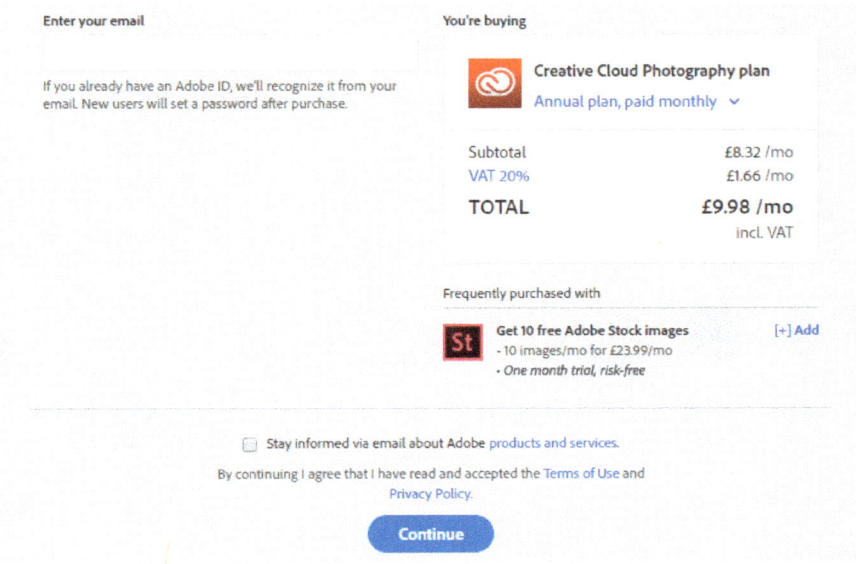

Chapter 1: Getting Started with Photoshop

Once you're purchased Photoshop, go to your desktop apps catalog. In your web browser, navigate to the link below...

`www.adobe.com/creativecloud/catalog/desktop.html`

Scroll down the page, locate Photoshop and click 'download'.

This will download the Creative Cloud installer. Once it has downloaded, go to your downloads folder and double click on the file - which is usually 'CreativeCloudSetup.exe'.

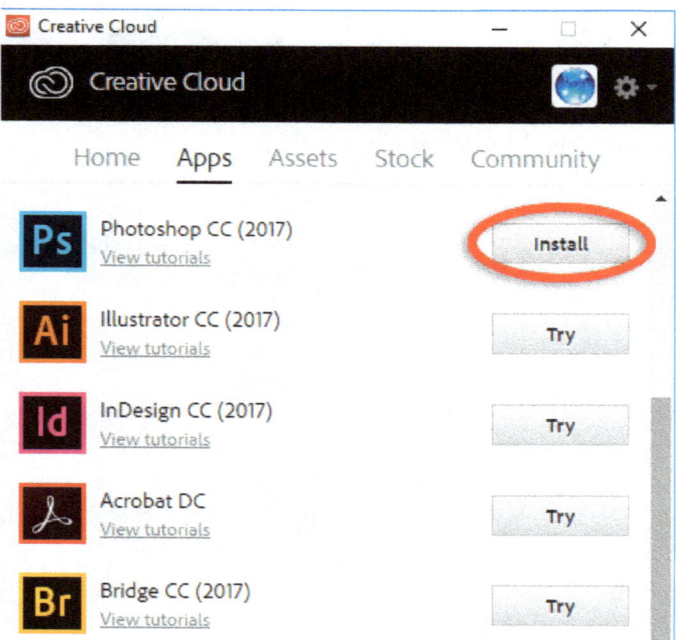

When the Creative Cloud app installs, select the 'apps' tab and click 'install' next to Photoshop CC.

Opening a Blank Project

Opening Photoshop, you'll see a thumbnail list of all your most recent projects. You can either open one of these or open a new blank project.

To open a new project, click 'create new' on the left hand side of your screen. Here you'll see some preset page sizes and templates.

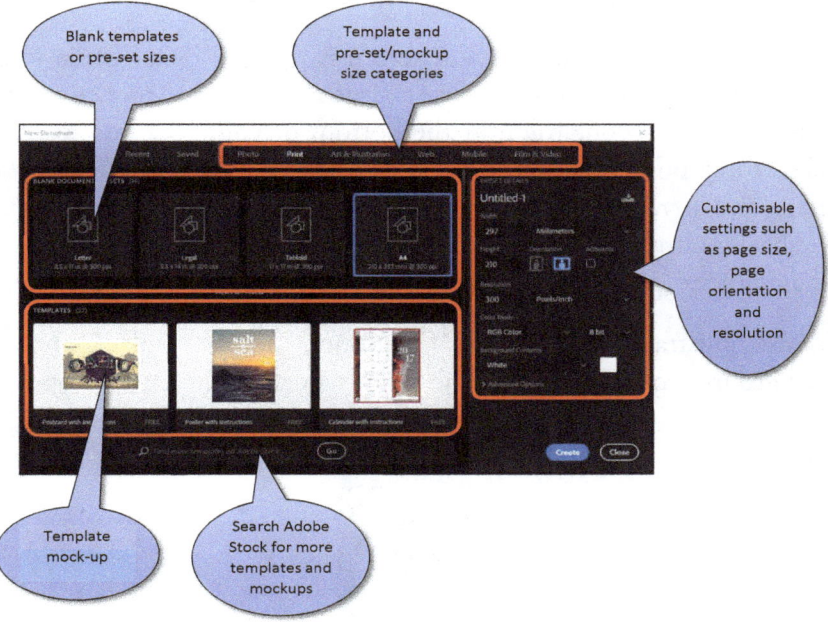

Blank templates or pre-set sizes

Template and pre-set/mockup size categories

Customisable settings such as page size, page orientation and resolution

Template mock-up

Search Adobe Stock for more templates and mockups

Chapter 1: Getting Started with Photoshop

Once you select a size, Photoshop will open a blank canvas for you to start your design.

Along the top of your screen you'll see the options bar, this changes depending on which tool is selected from the tool box. It allows you to change brush size, text size, colour and so on.

Along the left hand side of your screen is the tool box. This is where you'll find all your tools; the paint brush, eraser, pen tool, text tool, crop tool and so on. Right at the bottom of your tool box, you can select foreground colour - this is the colour of your paint brush, text, shape and anything you draw. The background colour is the colour of the background layer, the colour of the eraser tool and the end colour of a gradient (gradients go from foreground to background colour).

In the illustration below, the foreground colour is black and the background colour is white. The double sided arrow on the top right swaps the colours around.

Using a Template or Mockup

From Photoshop's start page, select 'create new' on the left hand side. From the pop up window, select a template or mock-up. In this example, I am going to use the magazine mock-up. You'll find this one under the 'print' category. Select the 'magazine mock-up' thumbnail, then click 'open'.

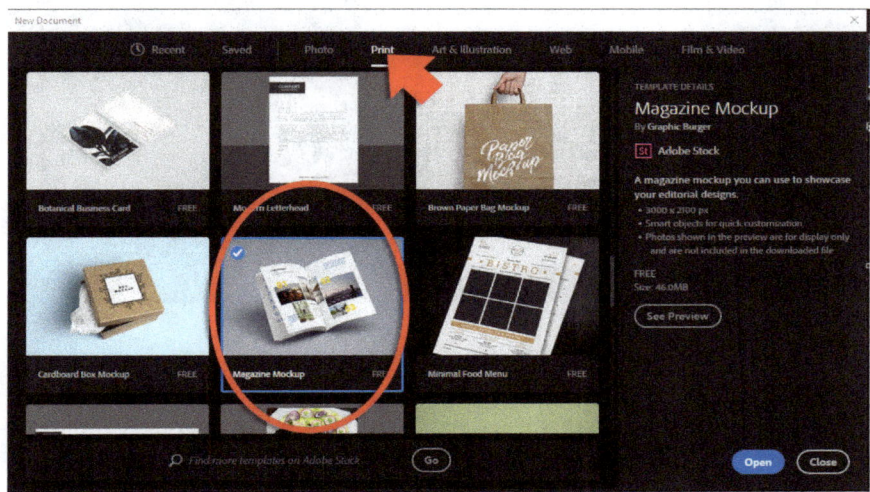

Now, you can customize this mock-up. In your layers pallet you'll see some highlighted layers. Double click on this to change the customization. In this case you can change the contents of the pages on the mock-up.

Chapter 1: Getting Started with Photoshop

In the window that opens up, drag and drop your own image/design onto the page. In this example, I am pasting in a sample book page.

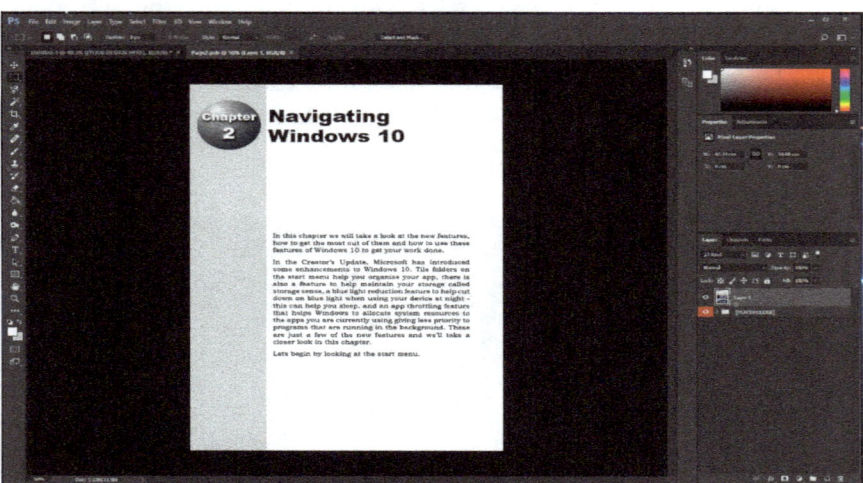

Close the window, click 'save' from the popup dialog box.

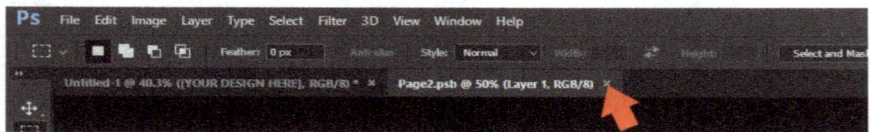

Do this will all the other highlighted layers.

Opening a Saved Project

When you start Photoshop, you'll see a screen with a thumbnail view of all your most recently opened projects and images. If you see your project here, just click on the thumbnail to open it up. If not click 'open' on the left hand side of your screen and browse for the project.

The project will open in the main window. Here you can edit and manipulate the image as you want using the various Photoshop tools

The Toolbox & Options Bar

In the Photoshop window, the toolbox appears on the left of the screen. As you can see, Photoshop has an enormous array of tools available. Many of these tools also have options that appear in the options bar at the top of the screen. So from the options bar you can change paint brush size and shape, or for the text tool you can change the font and colour etc.

For example, if I select the text tool from the toolbox, along the top of the screen, I have some options I can change such as font, size, colour and so on.

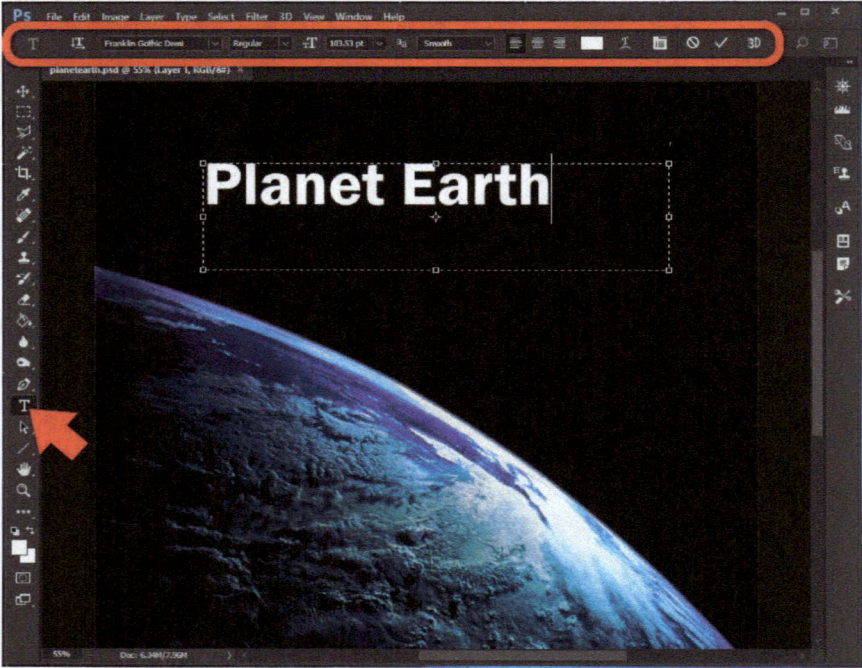

The options bar will display the options related to the tool selected from the toolbox.

Additional related tools are indicated by a small arrow at the bottom right of the tool icon.

If you click on a tool and hold your mouse button down for a second, you'll see these additional menus.

Rectangular Marquee Tool M	Move
Elliptical Marquee Tool M	Marque Selection
Single Row Marquee Tool	Lasso
Single Column Marquee Tool	Magic Wand
Lasso Tool L	Crop
Polygonal Lasso Tool L	Eye Dropper
Magnetic Lasso Tool L	Spot Healing
Quick Selection Tool W	Brush & Pencils
Magic Wand Tool W	Clone Stamp
Crop Tool C	History Brush
Perspective Crop Tool C	Eraser & BG Eraser
Slice Tool C	Gradient & Paint Bucket
Slice Select Tool C	Smudge & Sharpen
Eyedropper Tool I	Dodge & Burn Tools
3D Material Eyedropper Tool I	Pen & Anchor Points
Color Sampler Tool I	Text
Ruler Tool I	Path Selection
Note Tool I	Custom Shapes
Count Tool I	Grab & Rotate
Pen Tool P	Zoom
Freeform Pen Tool P	Foreground and Background Colour
Add Anchor Point Tool	
Delete Anchor Point Tool	
Convert Point Tool	
Horizontal Type Tool T	
Vertical Type Tool T	
Horizontal Type Mask Tool T	
Vertical Type Mask Tool T	
Path Selection Tool A	
Direct Selection Tool A	

Spot Healing Brush Tool J
Healing Brush Tool J
Patch Tool J
Content-Aware Move Tool J
Red Eye Tool J
Brush Tool B
Pencil Tool B
Color Replacement Tool B
Mixer Brush Tool B
Clone Stamp Tool S
Pattern Stamp Tool S
History Brush Tool Y
Art History Brush Tool Y
Eraser Tool E
Background Eraser Tool E
Magic Eraser Tool E
Gradient Tool G
Paint Bucket Tool G
3D Material Drop Tool G
Blur Tool
Sharpen Tool
Smudge Tool
Dodge Tool O
Burn Tool O
Sponge Tool O
Rectangle Tool U
Rounded Rectangle Tool U
Ellipse Tool U
Polygon Tool U
Line Tool U
Custom Shape Tool U
Hand Tool H
Rotate View Tool R

Pen Tool

The pen tool creates precise paths that can be manipulated using anchor points.

Crop Tool

The crop tool can be used to select a particular area of an image and discard the portions outside of the chosen section. A crop creates a focal point on an image, excluding unnecessary or excess space. Click and drag the cursor around the desired area, hit enter and the area outside of the rectangle is the discarded.

Slice Tool

The slice tool is used in isolating parts of an image. The slice tool can be used to divide an image into different sections, and these separate parts can be used as pieces of a web page.

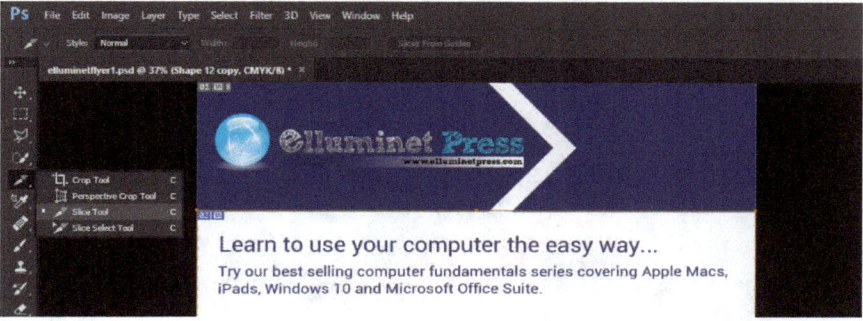

The slice select tool allows sliced sections of an image to be adjusted and shifted.

Move Tool

Once an area of an image is highlighted with the marquee tool, the move tool can be used to manually relocate the selected piece to anywhere on the canvas.

Marquee Tool

The marquee tool can make selections that are single row, single column, rectangular and elliptical. An area that has been selected can be edited without affecting the rest of the image. Once the tool has been selected, dragging across the desired area will select it. The selected area will be outlined by dotted lines, referred to as "marching ants".

Lasso Tool

The lasso tool is similar to the marquee tool; however, you can make a custom selection by drawing it freehand. There are three options for the lasso tool – regular, polygonal, and magnetic.

The regular lasso tool allows you to trace around your selection freehand. Photoshop will complete the selection once the mouse button is released. You can also complete the selection by connecting the end point to the starting point. The "marching ants" will indicate if a selection has been made.

The polygonal lasso tool will only draw straight lines, which makes it an ideal choice for images with many straight lines. Unlike the regular lasso tool, you must continually click around the image to outline the shape. To complete the selection, you must connect the end point to the starting point just like the regular lasso tool.

Magnetic lasso tool is considered the smart tool. It can do the same as the other two, but it can also detect the edges of an image once the user selects a starting point. It detects the edge of an object by examining difference in pixels as the cursor move over the desired area. Closing the selection is the same as the other two, which should also should display the "marching ants" once the selection has been closed.

Quick Selection Tool

The quick selection tool selects areas based on edges, similarly to the magnetic lasso tool. The difference between this tool and the lasso tool is that there is no starting and ending point. Since there isn't a starting and ending point, the selected area can be added on to as much as possible without starting over.

By dragging the cursor over the desired area, the quick selection tool detects the edges of the image. The "marching ants" tell you what is currently being selected. Once done, the selected area can be edited without affecting the rest of the image.

Magic Wand

The magic wand tool selects areas based on pixels of a similar colour and intensity. You only need to click once, and this tool will detect pixels that are very similar to each other. When the image requires more than a few clicks, this tool doesn't work particularly well.

Eraser

The eraser tool will convert the pixels to transparent, unless it is the background layer. The size and style of the eraser can be selected in the options bar. This tool is unique in that it can take the form of the paintbrush and pencil tools.

In addition to the straight eraser tool, there are two more available options – background eraser and magic eraser. The background eraser deletes any part of the image that is on the edge of an object. This tool is often used to extract objects from the background.

The magic eraser tool deletes based on similar coloured pixels. It is very similar to the magic wand tool.

This tool is ideal for deleting areas with the same colour or tone that contrasts with the rest of the image.

Text Tool

The text tool creates an area on a new layer where text can be entered, and creates vector-based text, so symbols, letters and numbers in various fonts and colours can be re-sized while maintaining the same quality.

Retouch Tool

There are several tools that are used for retouching, manipulating and adjusting photos, such as the clone stamp, eraser, burn, dodge, smudge and blur tools.

The clone stamp tool samples a selected portion of an image, and duplicates it over another area using a brush that can be adjusted in size, flow and opacity.

The smudge tool, smudges the image when dragged over as if it was water colour paint.

The blur tool softens portions of an image by blurring the area.

The burn and dodge tools, which are derived from traditional methods of adjusting the exposure on printed photos, have opposite effects; the burn tool darkens selected areas, and the dodge tool lightens them.

Healing Tools

With retouching tools like the clone stamp tool and healing brush tool, imperfections of an image can easily be removed. These tools essentially function by locating a source point or multiple source points that can be scaled or rotated in order to cover an imperfection or unwanted detail in a specific area of an image.

The clone stamp tool allows you to replace one part of an image with another. If part of an original image is damaged, the damaged area can be restored by cloning a similar area from within the same image. This tool works great for removing unwanted blemishes.

To sample part of the image to be cloned, hold down the Alt key (PC) or the Option key (Mac) then click on the area.

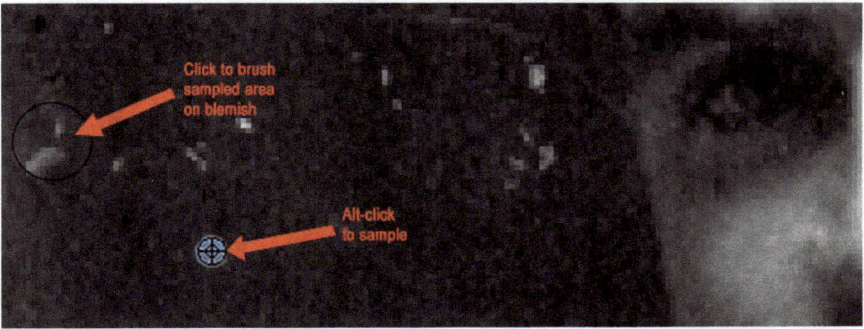

Once the sample area has been cloned, click the area of the photo to be restored - use the tool like a paint brush and 'paint' over the blemishes. You can change the size of the clone area from the options bar. Just select brush size and hardness.

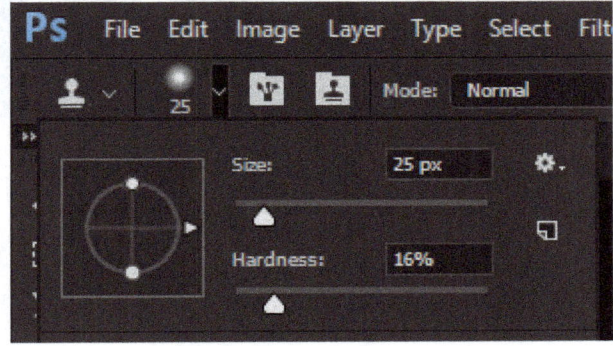

Custom Shapes

Custom shapes allows you to create different types of shapes such as squares, rectangles and ellipses, as well as polygons with 3 sides or more such as triangles, pentagons, hexagons and so on.

Select the polygon tool, it's on the shapes tool - click and hold your mouse button on the icon on the toolbox for a second to reveal the menu. From this menu, you can select a standard square/rectangle, ellipse or polygon. For this example, I selected 'polygon tool'.

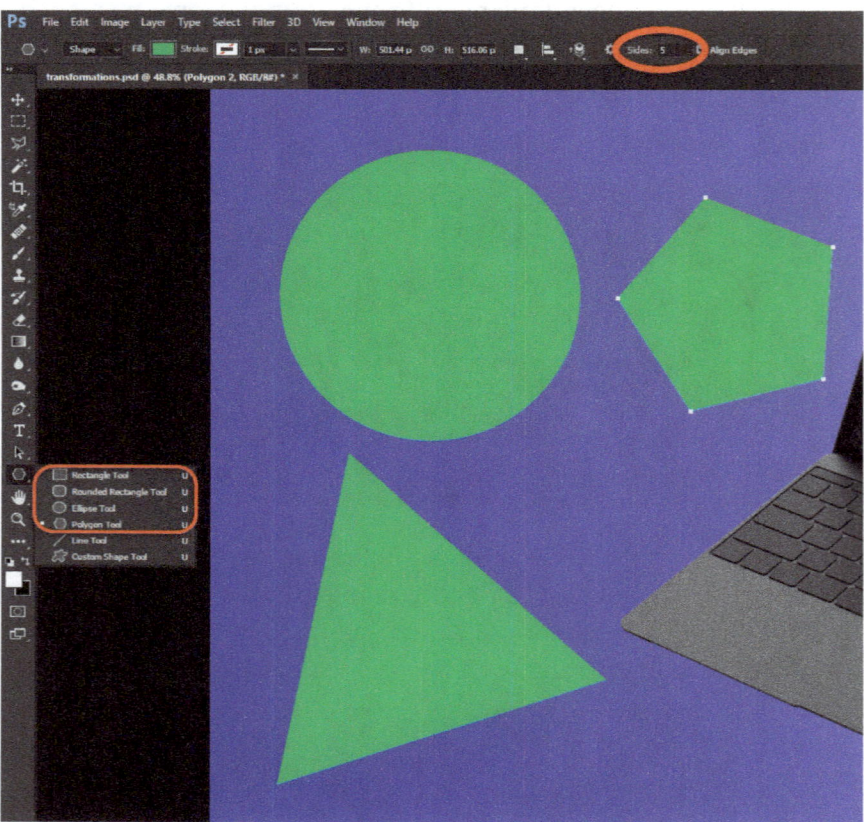

Notice in the options bar at the top of the screen, you can change the fill colour as well as the number of sides your polygon has.

You can also change the stroke colour (outline) from the options bar.

Give it a try.

Photoshop also has some custom shapes such as arrows and decorative shapes you can use.

From the shapes tool on the toolbox, click and hold your mouse for a second to reveal the menu. Select 'custom shapes tool'.

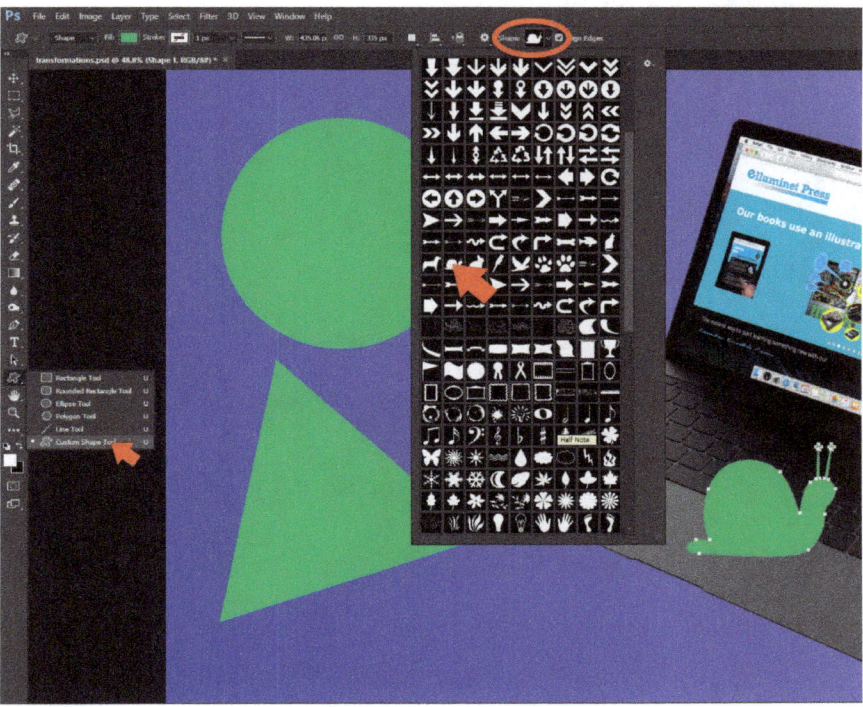

Click and drag your mouse on the canvas to create your shape.

To maintain the shape's aspect ratio, hold down the shift key while you click and drag your mouse on the canvas to create your shape - this prevents the shape from being stretched or squashed.

Pencils & Brushes

Pencils and brushes allow you to draw freehand illustrations and make minor touch ups to images. Select the paint brush tool from the tool box. You can change the size, shape and hardness of the brush on the options bar at the top of the screen.

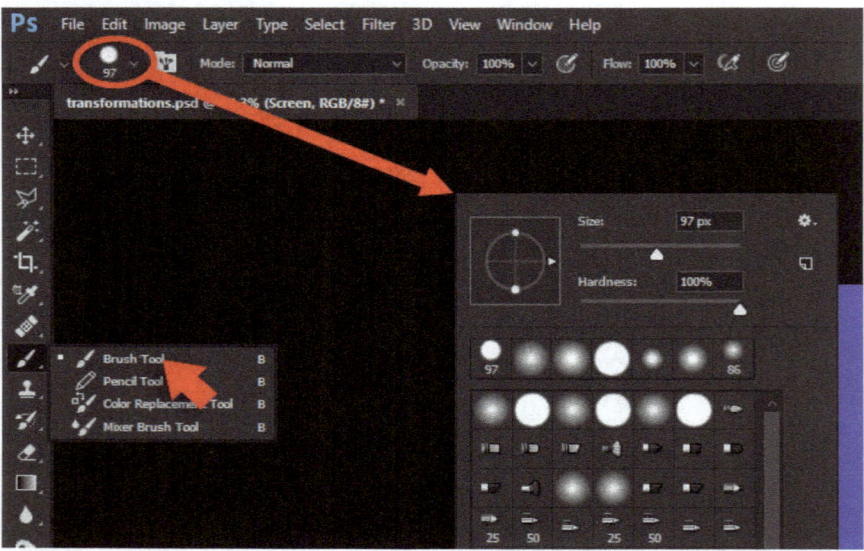

Size is the thickness of the brush, while hardness is how much the brush feathers at the edges.

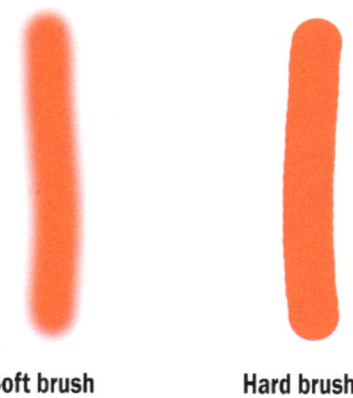

Soft brush   **Hard brush**

Change the colour of the brush using the colour selector at the bottom of the toolbox on the left hand side.

You can change the shape of the brush too. Open the brush panel from the options bar and on the top left, drag the two small white dots on the brush to change the shape.

Underneath that you can select some preset brush styles. Click on them and try them out. You can also load up more brush styles. To do this, click the cog icon on the top right of the brush style panel.

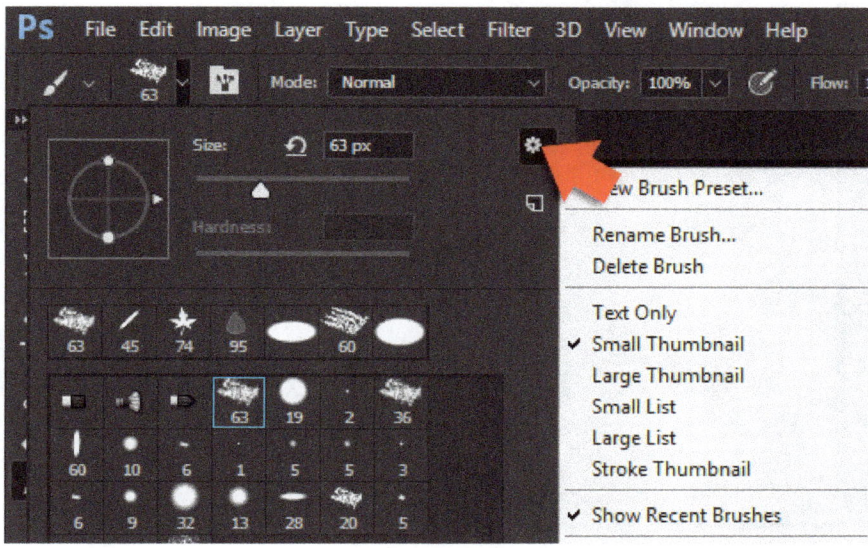

Right down at the bottom of the menu are some sets of brushes, click on then to add the brush types to the list. Give them a try.

Draw directly onto the canvas with your brush. A good accessory to use when drawing freehand is a graphics tablet.

Eye Dropper

You can use the eye dropper tool to sample a colour on an image, layer or object.

Click and hold your mouse on a particular colour you want to sample, and you'll see the sample ring. The outside colour is a neutral grey which is meant to help you distinguish the colours. On the inner ring, the top half is the colour you just sampled, and the bottom half is the previous colour you sampled. Your sampled colour will appear as the foreground colour on the bottom of your toolbox.

Panels

You can find your panels displayed down the right hand side of your screen. These panels contain adjustments and customizations for your tools. The default layout will look similar to the ones below.

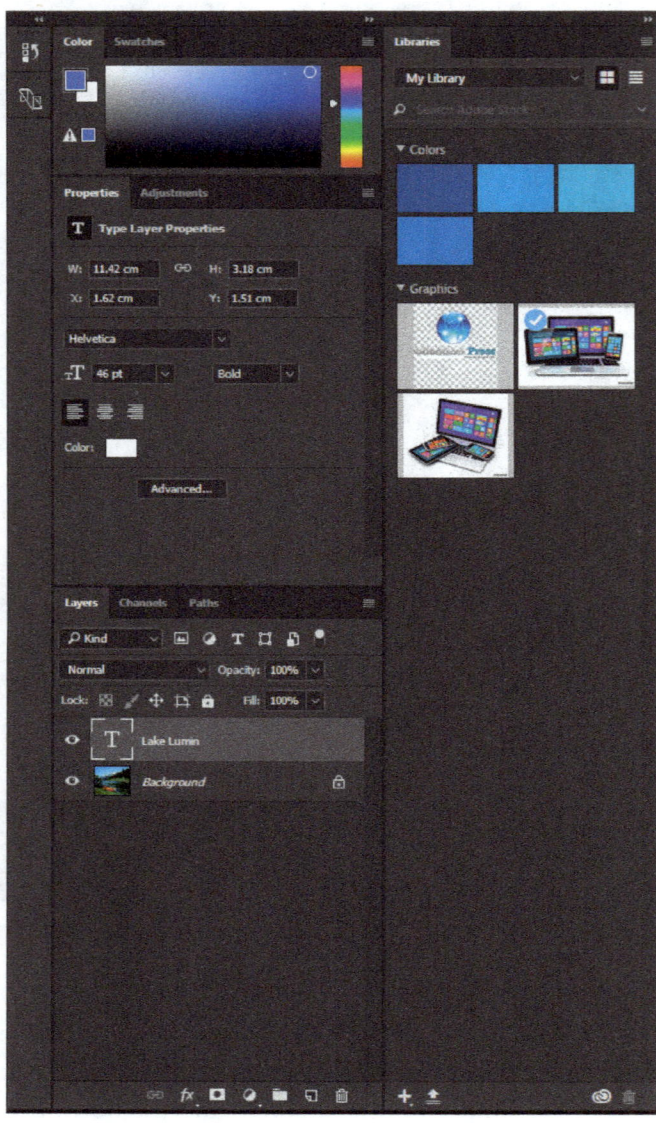

Here you'll find all your options to make adjustments for your tools such as, text size, layers, blending, and so on.

Opening & Closing Panels

Most tools have a panel with adjustments and customizations, but they don't all open up at the same time. You can open panels from the 'window' menu.

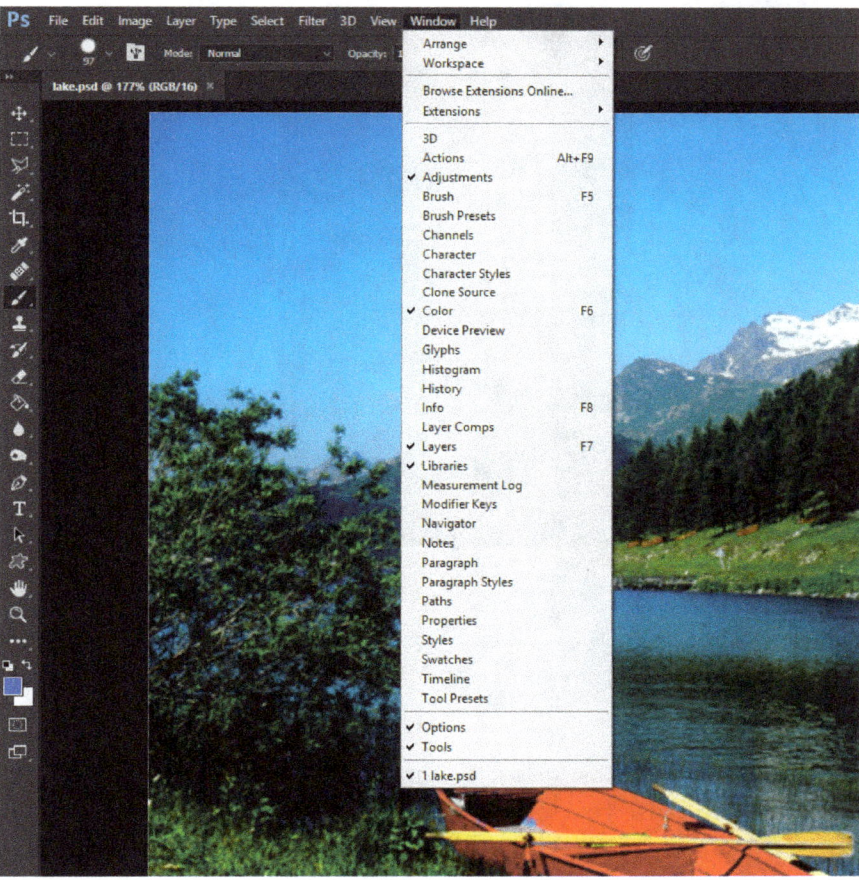

Panels that are currently open will have a tick next to the name in the 'window' menu.

Layers Panel

One of the most important panels is the layers panel. This is where you'll build up your design, collage and effects in your projects.

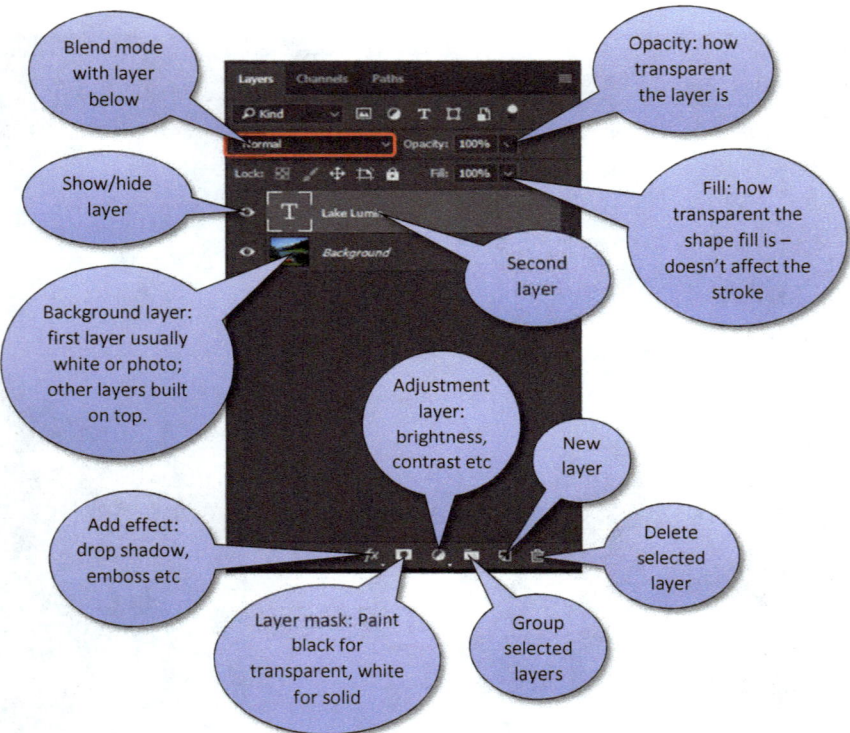

We'll take a closer look at layers in more detail later in this guide, but for now, familiarize yourself with the icons on the panel and what they do.

2 Common Tasks

In this chapter we'll be looking at some common tasks performed using Photoshop.

For these examples, you'll need to download the Photoshop resources from the Photoshop Resources section on the website.

`www.elluminetpress.com/resources`

Select the Photoshop Basics book cover.

Download and unpack the zip file into your pictures directory.

Import Images

The first step in preparing to use Photoshop is to import a digital image. Although you can use Photoshop's drawing tools to create graphics from scratch.

There are a number of ways to obtain digital images:

- Scanners

- Digital cameras

These can be found in the file > import menu. In the example below I'm importing an image from a scanner.

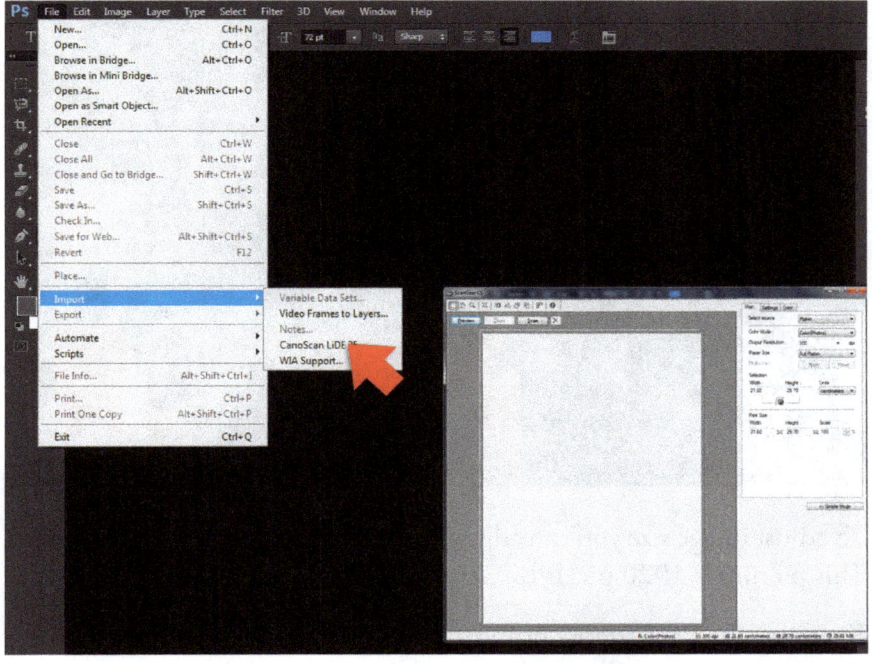

If your image already exists as a file then go to file -> open

Change Image Size

The image size menu allows you to view and adjust pixel information, document size and resolution.

The following example uses the **flower.jpg** file in your pictures folder.

Click on the image menu then select 'image size'.

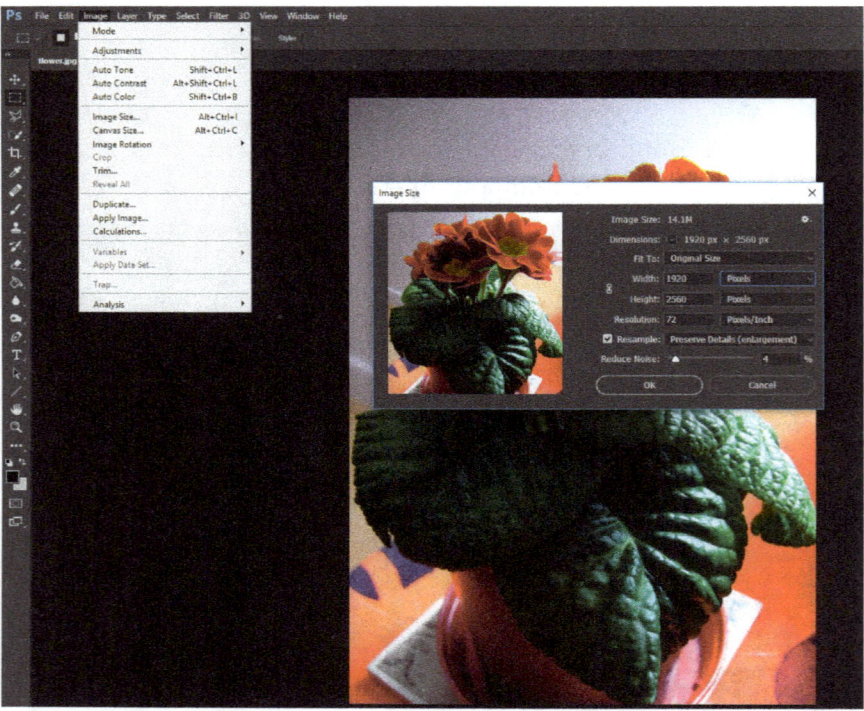

To adjust image size you can adjust the pixel dimensions in this window. This picture is 1920 pixels by 2560 pixels.

Keeping the 'constrain proportions' box checked, allows you to change either the width or height of the image while maintaining the proportionate size of the picture (the aspect ratio).

If it's easier you can also change the picture size at a percentage by changing the pixels drop down box to percentage. You can also select centimeters or inches if you prefer.

Rotate an Image

Sometimes photos need to be rotated; perhaps you took a photo in portrait mode, as shown below, but has been imported "side ways". It is easy to rotate and flip images in Photoshop.

Go to the image menu and select 'image rotation'.

You can rotate your images using some presets, these are:

- 180° (rotates image 180°)

- 90° CW (rotates clockwise - as in above example)

- 90° CCW (rotates anti-clockwise)

- Arbitrary – lets you choose the angle, eg 45°

Also you can mirror image your photos or images by flipping them horizontally or vertically. These work great for creating reflection effects.

Flip Horizontally

Flip Vertically

Crop an Image

Use the crop tool to crop an image or photo. This can improve the appearance of your image by re-framing or removing unwanted parts of a photo, as well as decrease the file size.

For this example, we will use **molly.jpg**

From the toolbox, select the crop tool.

Select the area you wish to keep by clicking and dragging the highlighted rectangle around the area. Notice how the area you want to keep is highlighted, but the area to be discarded is dimmed.

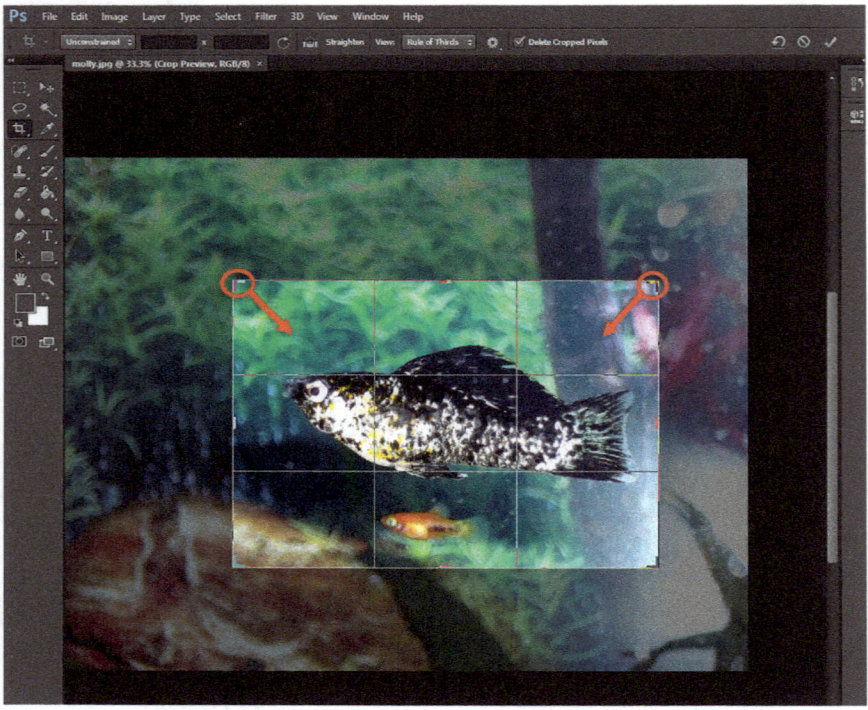

To resize the crop box, click and drag the corners around the area you want to keep.

Double-click in the centre of the highlighted area. This removes the area outside of the crop box.

Content Aware Crop

Content aware fills the areas outside the original image when you perform a reverse crop. Photoshop will make a best guess based on the background of your image.

Select the crop tool from the toolbox on the left hand side. Along the bar at the top you'll see an option called 'content aware'. Click the tick box next to the option to enable it.

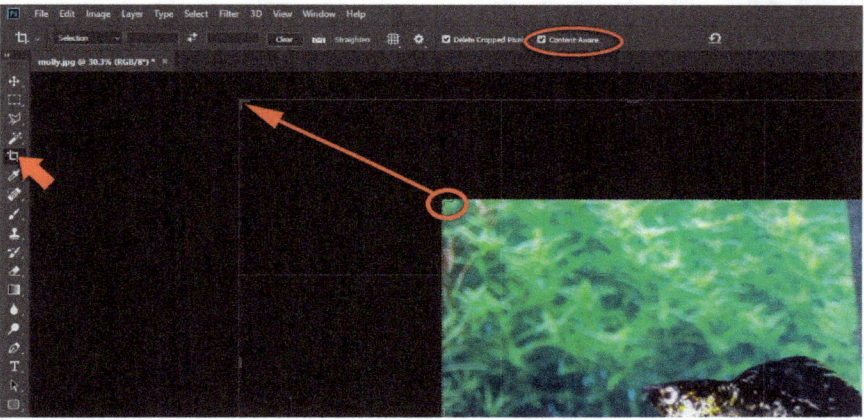

Now drag the corner crop handle outwards to enlarge the crop. Hit the tick icon on the bar at the top to execute the crop.

See how Photoshop has continued the background pattern on the image on the right.

Adjust an Image

Under the image menu, there is a slideout menu called 'adjustments'. This menu has a several adjustment controls that can improve the look and feel of your image.

To work with these tools, lets open the file **daffodils.jpg**

Go to the image menu, select 'adjustments', and then click 'levels'.

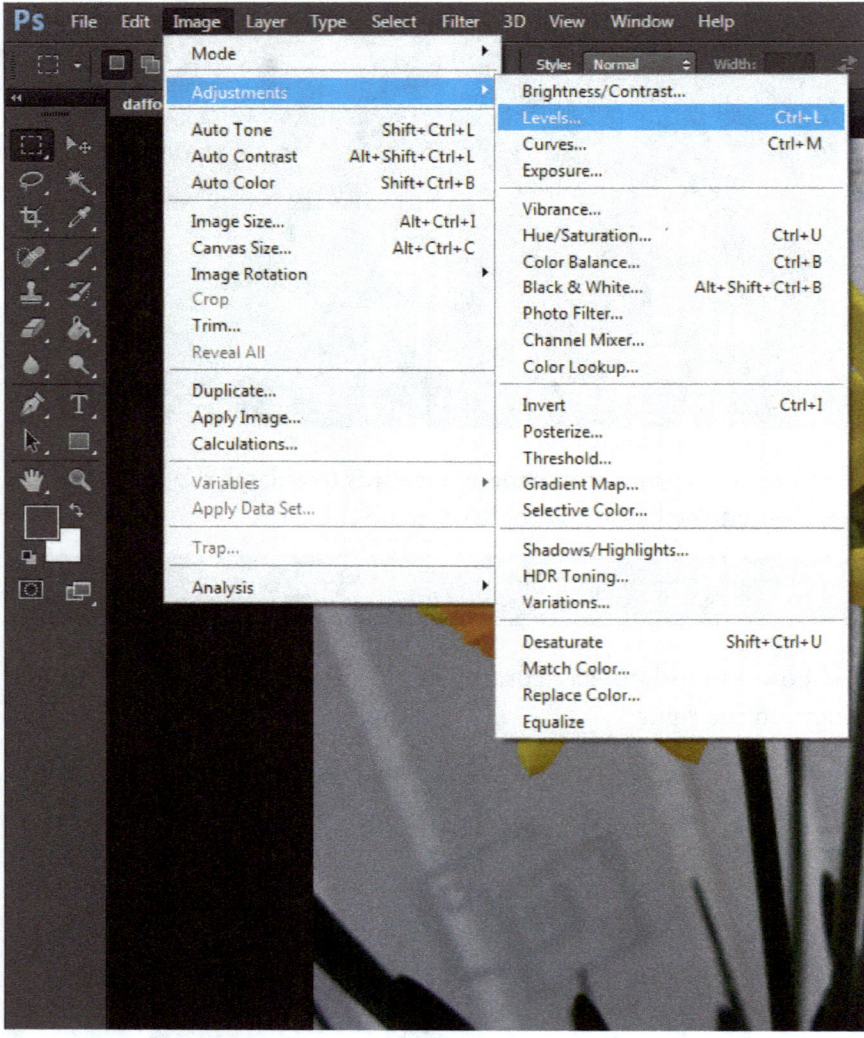

Click 'auto' in the dialog box. Photoshop now will analyse the image and adjust the colour, contrast and colour balance for you.

Auto levels changes the brightness, contrast, colour setting, highlights, and shadows.

Sometimes the auto adjust doesn't always get it right. You can manually adjust the image with the histogram sliders marked below.

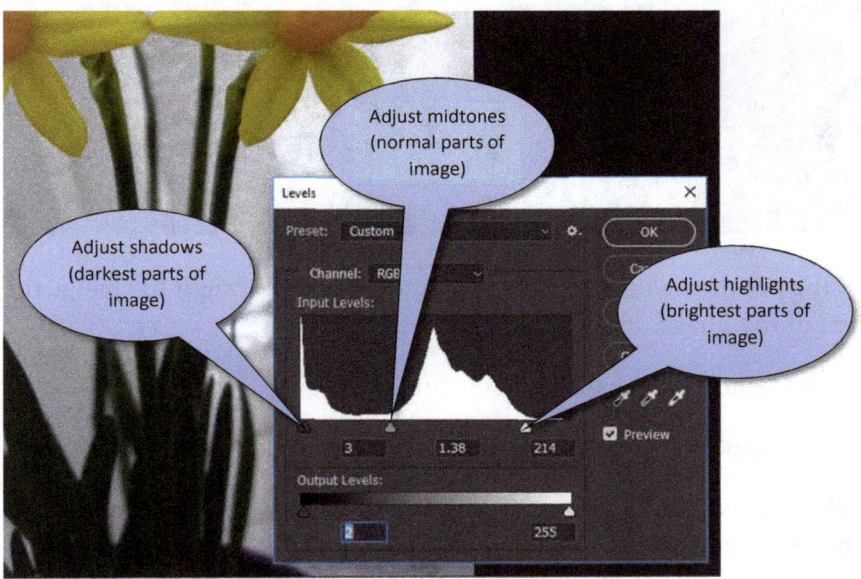

Give it a try and see what happens.

Hue and Saturation levels

We can also adjust the image using the hue/saturation levels, or curves. This adjusts the tint, intensity and brightness of your colours. For example, lets change the colour of the daffodils.

Open the **daffodils.jpg** image and save it as a Photoshop file in your pictures folder.

Open the hue/saturation window under the images/adjustments menu.

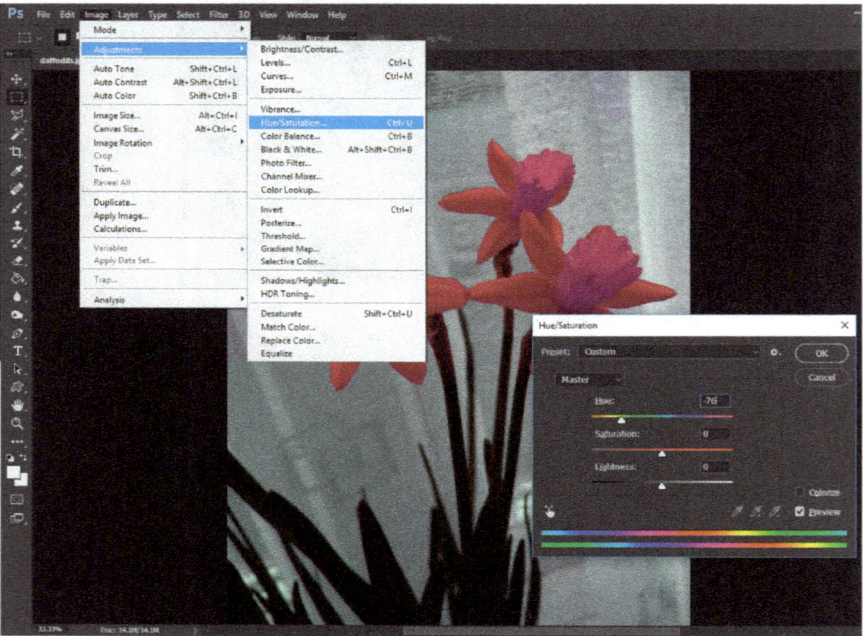

In the popup dialog box, move the hue slider left or right to change the hue of the image. How about purple daffodils?

Experiment with the different channels: RGB.

What happens when you move the saturation and lightness sliders?

Click where it says 'master', you can change the hue of the reds or greens in the photograph etc.

Brightness and Contrast

The brightness/contrast tool is extremely useful for making adjustments to the lighting.

Open the **brighton.jpg** image.

Go to image menu and select 'adjustments'. From the slideout, select 'brightness/contrast'.

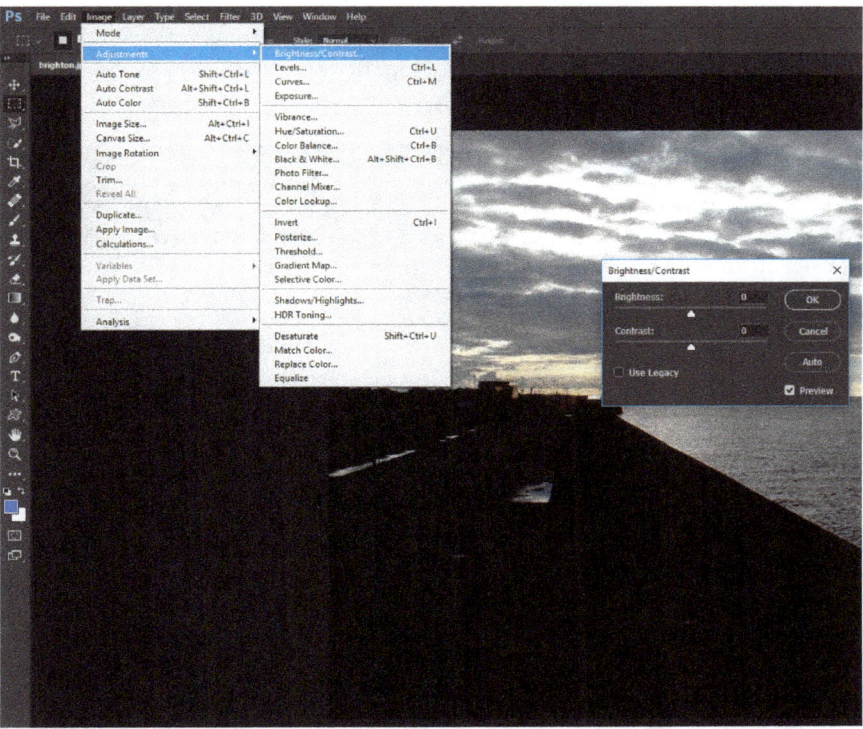

Move the brightness slider to the right to lighten the picture.

Move the contrast slider to the left to add back some of the picture's detail in the shadows.

Shadows and Highlights

There is another way to adjust picture brightness that may work better for photos with underexposed areas. Under the image/adjustments menu, there is an option called shadows/highlights. This option allows you to lighten areas that are dark due to shadows and add back some detail in the brighter parts of the images.

To work with these tools, let's open **brighton.jpg**.

Go to the image menu, select 'adjustments'. From the slideout menu select 'shadows/highlights'. Photoshop now will open a window and automatically reduce shadows by 50%.

We can change the amount of shadow by moving the slider left or right. Moving the slider completely to the right removes 100% of the shadows. Notice the additional detail on the road. At the same time, the sky remains cloudy, rather than being bright and washed out as when only using the brightness control.

The highlight control allows you to darken and bring out some of the detail in the brighter parts of the picture. Use these controls sparingly.

Free Transform Tool

The free transform tools allows you to resize, distort or rotate an image, object or shape on a particular layer.

For this exercise, open up **transformations.psd**

You can transform any object or image. To do this make sure you have selected the layer that the image or object is on in the layers panel on the right hand side.

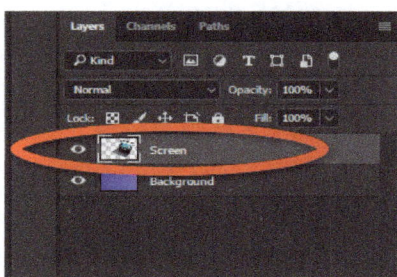

Once you have done that, select the marquee tool from your tool box.

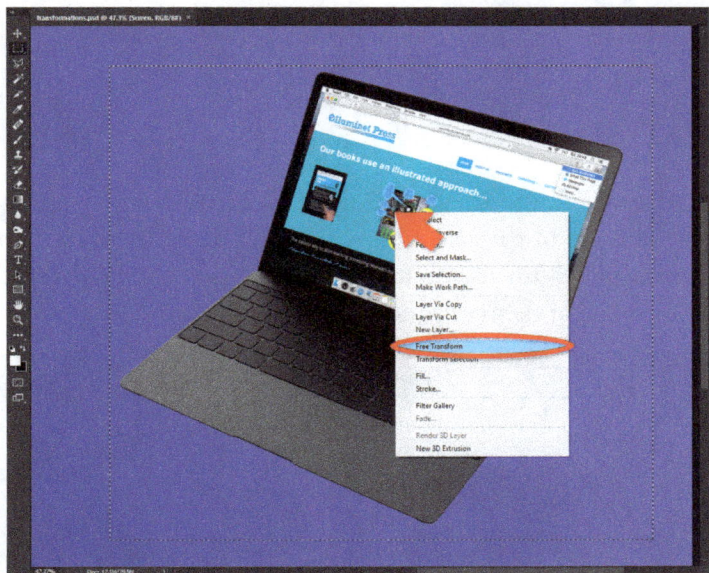

Click and drag the box around the object, then right click your mouse on the selection. From the popup menu, select 'free transform'.

Now, you'll notice some resize handles appear around the selection. Click and drag these to resize your object. In this example, I am making the laptop image smaller.

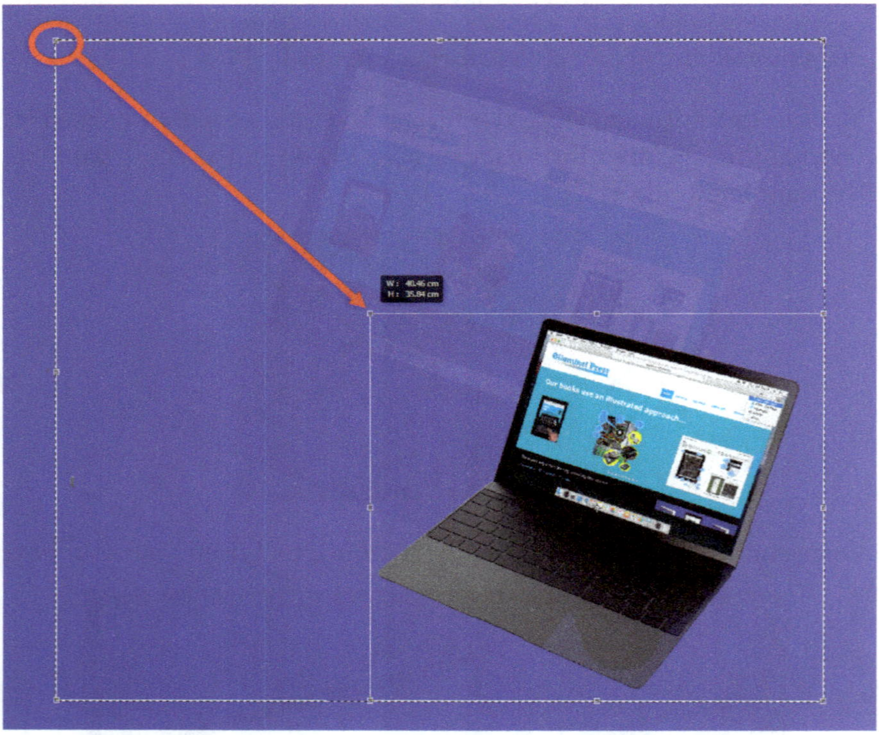

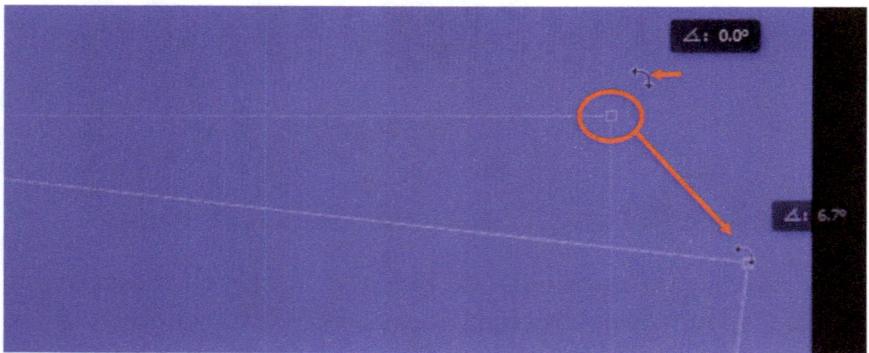

You can also rotate the image. To do this, hover your mouse around one of the corners of the selection. Click and drag the resize handle in the direction you want to rotate the image - you'll see a gauge appear with the number of degrees rotated.

If you right click on your selection again, you'll see a transform menu. This has some preset functions such as distort, perspective and so on.

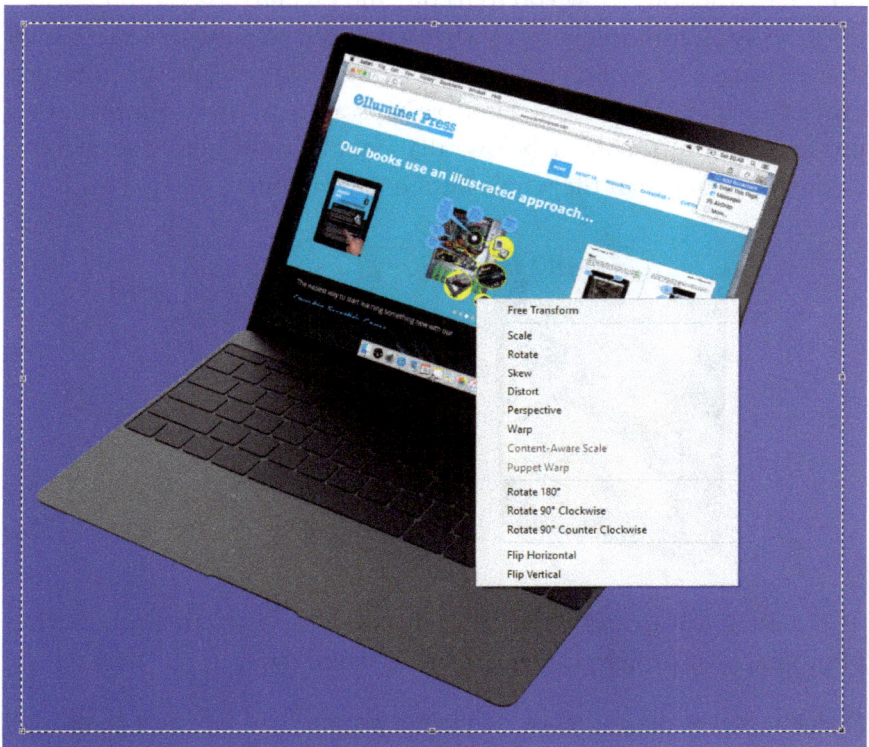

Try out some of these options. Try 'warp', 'skew', 'distort', or 'perspective' and see what they do.

Automated Actions

Automated actions allow you to record and execute tasks automatically, for processing multiple images when you need to apply the same steps to each image or when you need to automatically build a Photoshop project to give to someone else; perhaps a book cover template or a product mockup, shown below, that would only need the artwork changing rather than the whole design and layout.

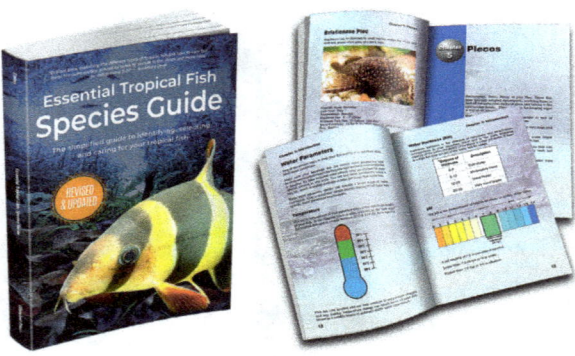

The action feature will record each step you take to process your photograph or project which can be 'replayed' later

Perhaps you want to resize or crop a whole load of high resolution photos from your favourite DSLR camera to email to friends, post on social media or use on a website. It would be very time consuming to do them all manually.

In this example, I'm going to resize the photos to make them easier to send to people. Open the image **clownloachhighres.jpg**.

The list of steps in this procedure are

1. Image > Image Size

2. Set width to 1024 pixels

3. Set resolution to 300dpi

4. Click OK

5. File > Save As

To create a new action, click the 'window' menu and select 'actions'. This will open the actions panel on the right hand side.

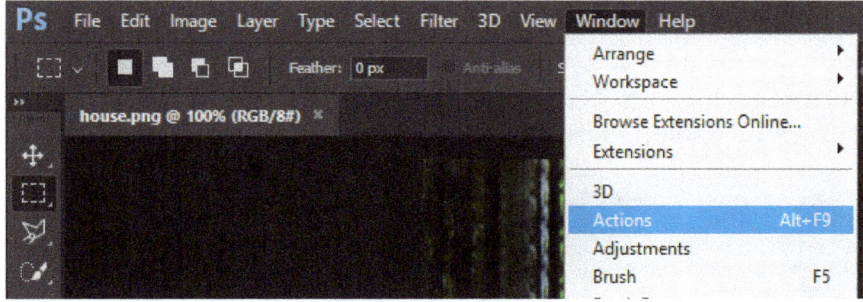

Click the 'new action' icon on the bottom right of the panel.

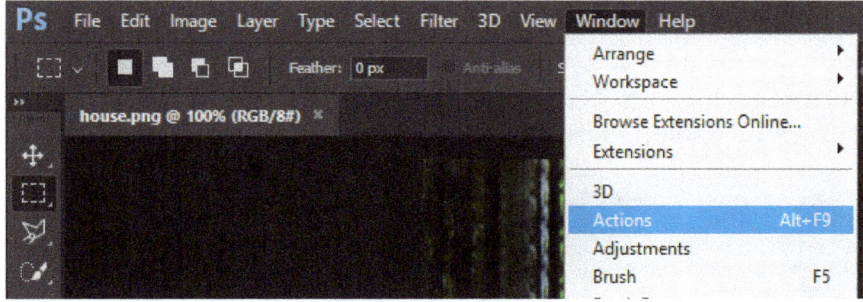

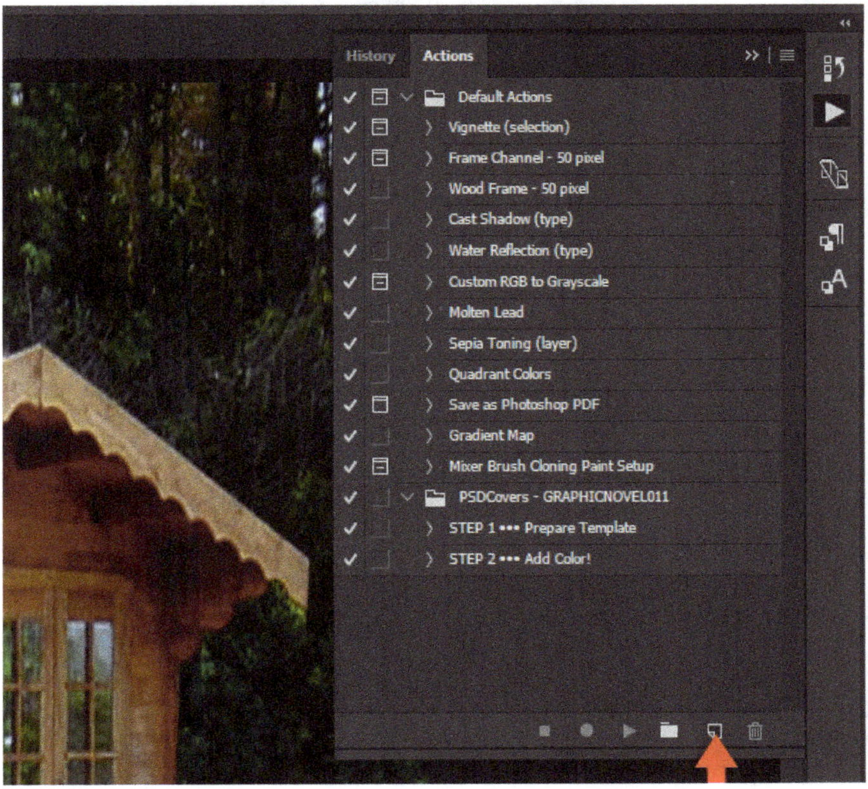

Give your new action a meaningful name when prompted then click OK. Photoshop will now be in record mode.

Any action you take in Photoshop will now be recorded. This is where you can now run through the procedure or steps you want to record in your 'action'.

Now we need to run through the procedure to resize the image. From the 'image' menu, select 'image size'. Adjust the width to 1024 pixels and set the resolution to 300, then click ok.

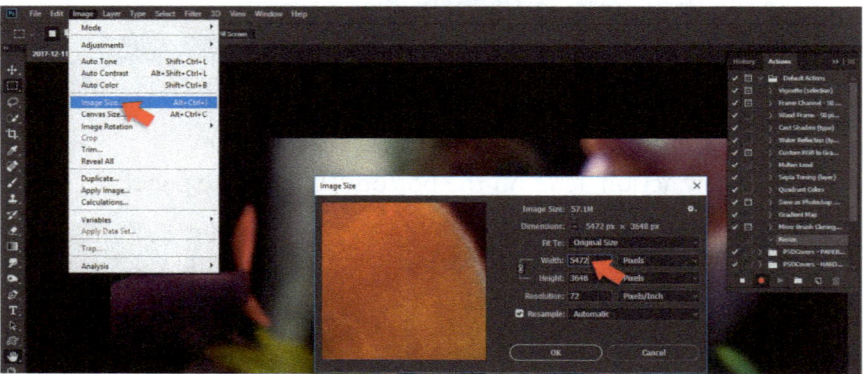

Next we want to save the processed image. So click the 'file' menu then select 'save as'.

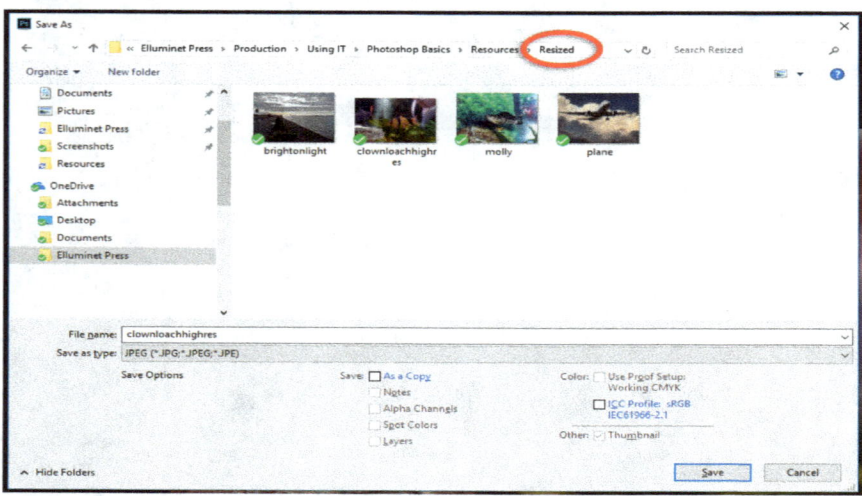

Create a new folder called 'resized' and save the processed image in there. *On a windows machine, just right click and select new folder from the popup menu. Click 'new folder' if you're on a Mac.*

Click the stop icon on the bottom of the actions panel. You'll see your action added to the actions panel.

To run the action, you can open any image and execute the action and it will resize any image to 1024 pixels (as we resized during recording).

Notice that this only works with one image... What happens if we had 1000 images to resize? This is where batch processing comes in. Have a look at the next section.

Batch Processing

Batch processing allows you to automate actions when you have a lot of images to process.

You can find the batch processing on the file menu.

File > Automate > Batch.

From the top left of the dialog box, select your action. In this example, I'm going to use the resize action we created in the previous section.

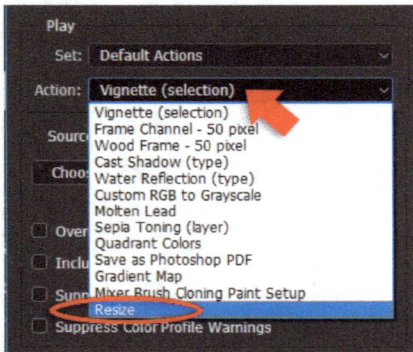

Select the folder where your images have been saved. In this example, I am resizing some photos I saved in my pictures folder from my DSLR camera.

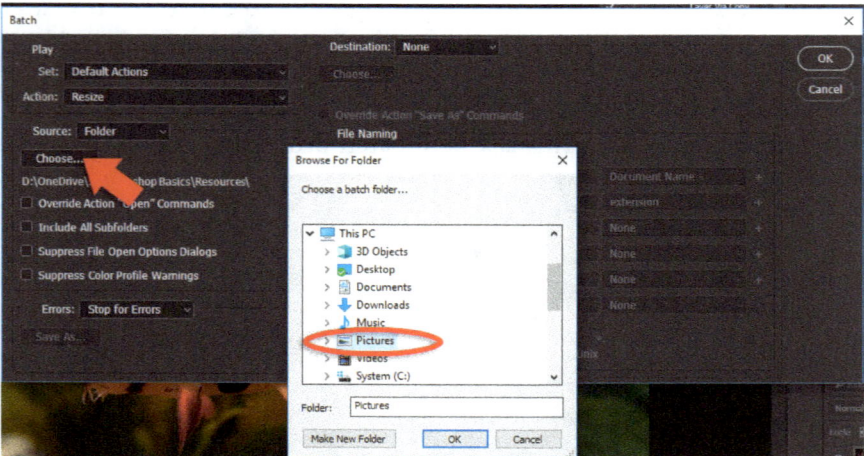

Change the destination drop down menu to 'folder'. This is where you want to save the resized images. Click 'choose', the browse and select the folder from the popup window. It makes sense to save these into a separate folder. I'm going to save them in to a folder called 'resized'. If the folder doesn't exist, click 'make new folder'.

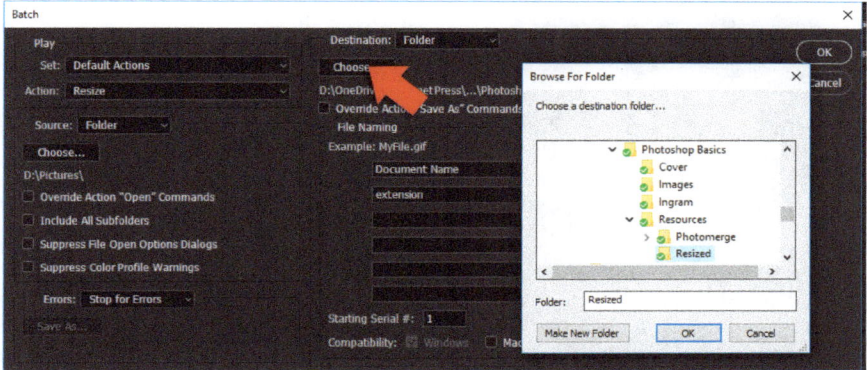

The original resize action already has a 'save as' step, but for batch processing, you're better off overriding the 'save as' step. This gives you more control over naming and directory output. To do this, click the checkbox next to 'override action save as commands'

3 Touching up Images

Photoshop can be used to touch up, enhance and edit photographs and images; whether these are taken with a camera or created within Photoshop.

Photoshop has a vast array of tools and filters for you to use. In this chapter, we'll take a look at some of the most common tools and filters you can apply to your work.

For the demonstrations in this chapter, you'll need to download the resource files from the Photoshop section at...

www.elluminetpress.com/resources

...and extract them to your photos folder.

Burn Tool

The burn is used to darken an area.

Click and hold the cursor on the dodge tool in the toolbox. From the sub menu select the burn tool.

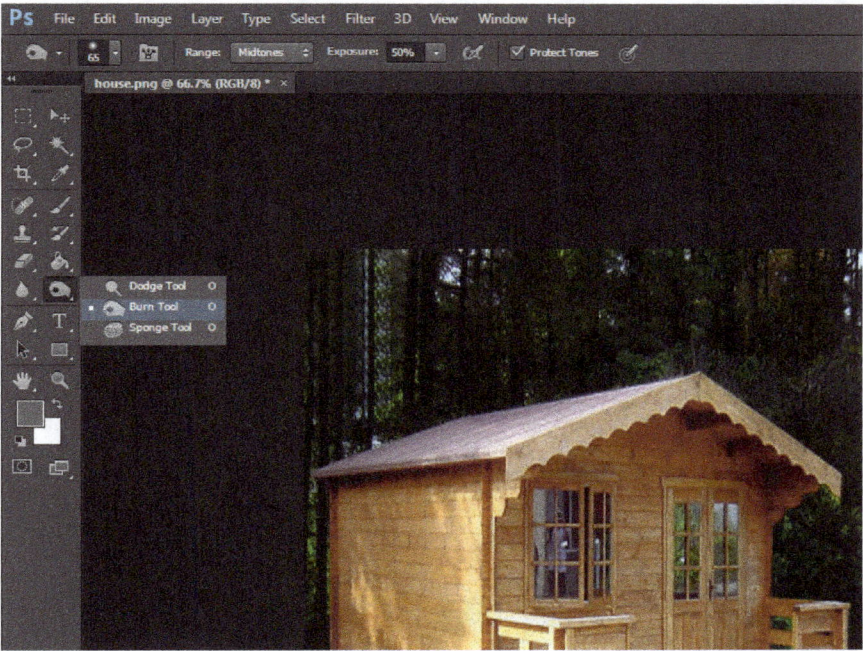

Images are divided into highlights, the bright parts of the image; mid tones and shadows. Since the part of the image we want to darken is a midtone/shadow, make sure you select 'midtones' from the range on the options bar at the top. If the section is too dark, try 'shadows'.

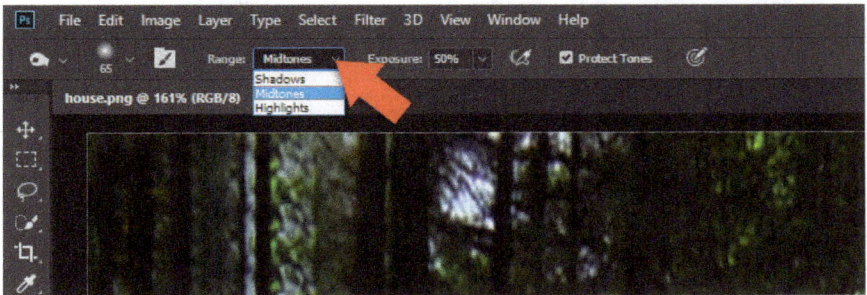

Chapter 3: Touching up Images

Select the size of the burn tool. The trees in the photo cover quite a large area, so a larger brush size would be better. Adjust the size slider and the hardness of the brush.

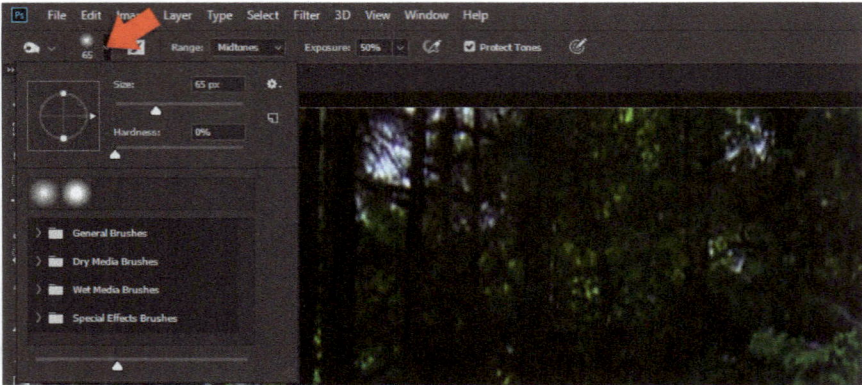

In the **house.png** image, use the burn tool to darken the trees in the background to make the cabin stand out more. Are these dark areas shadows or midtones? Try either of those settings and see what it does to the trees.

Notice how the midtones have been darkened, while the highlights haven't been touched.

If you wanted to darken the bright parts of the image, then select 'highlights' instead of 'midtones' from the 'range' drop down box on the toolbar.

Dodge Tool

The dodge tool works in the opposite way to the burn tool and can be used to lighten a dark area of a picture to bring out the detail.

Open the **house.png** image and use the dodge tool to lighten the path just in front of the house.

Images are divided into highlights, the bright parts of the image, mid tones and shadows. Since the part of the image we want to lighten is a midtone/shadow, make sure you select 'midtones' from the range on the options bar at the top. If the section is too dark, try 'shadows'.

Now click and rub the tool over the part of the image to lighten.

Heal Tool

Another useful tool is the heal tool. This tool uses samples in the surrounding area to replace the masked area of the image you selected.

In this example I'm going to use an old photograph that has been damaged.

Open **oldimage.jpg** image

Select the healing brush tool from the tool box. (It is grouped with the color replacement tool).

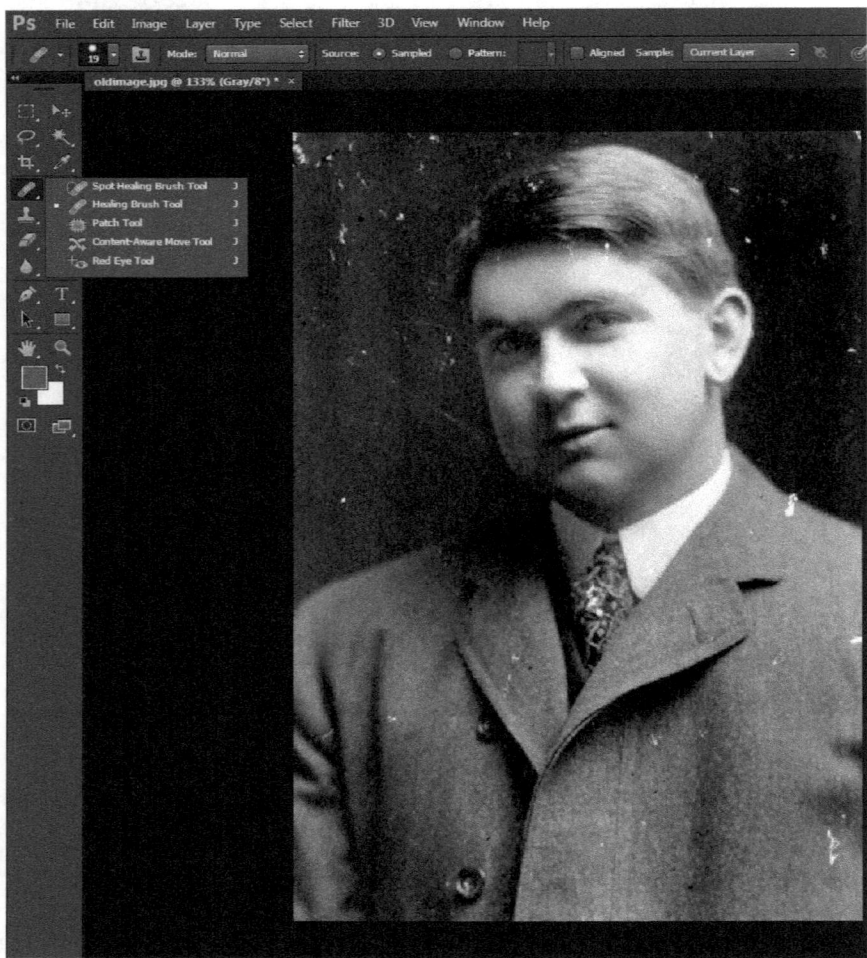

Alt-click on an area that is clean and free of any damaged parts. This will be used to as a "donor" to "heal" another area.

Now click on the area to be repaired. Best to sample as near to the damaged area as possible.

Continue clicking on areas to be repaired, selecting new "donor" areas as the content of the image changes.

Spot Healing Tool

Open the **brightonlight.jpg** image. Select the spot healing brush tool from your tool box.

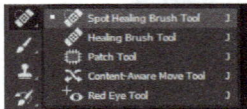

In this example, I'm going to use the spot healing tool to remove the sign post on the left hand side of the image. Click the brush size on the bar at the top of the screen, and adjust the size of the brush using the size slider to roughly the size of the sign we want to remove.

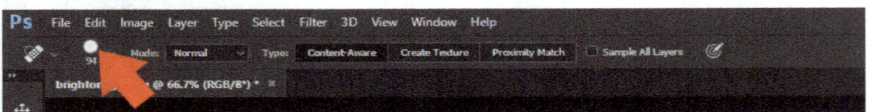

Along the top bar you'll see 'type'. This is the type of repair you want to perform. We'll use 'content aware' for this example. You can see the difference demonstrated below.

Content Aware   Create Texture   Proximity Match

'Content aware' analyses the surrounding area and attempts to interpret different parts of the image and generates a repair based on its analysis. This one usually produces the best results.

'Create texture' generates a texture based on the surrounding area and fills in the area to be repaired.

'Proximity match' samples the area surrounding the area to be repaired then generates a repair based on the data.

Now to repair the area, paint over the sign post as shown below.

When you release your mouse button, the area will be repaired.

Try experimenting with the three different types of the spot healing tool on different parts of the image. Try with content aware, create texture and proximity match. See what happens.

Content Aware Move Tool

Open the **brightonlight.jpg** image. In this image, say we wanted to move the bus a bit closer and a bit bigger in the image. First, select the content aware move tool from the healing brush section on your toolbox.

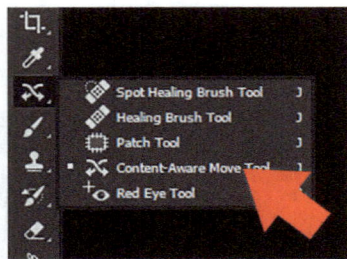

From the bar along the top of your screen set the 'mode' to 'move'.

'Move mode' cuts out your selection and fills in the original position. 'Extend mode' duplicates the selection.

Next trace around the bus in the image, as shown below

Drag your selection towards the left as shown below. You can resize the selection using the resize handles on the surrounding box.

You can see Photoshop has attempted to remove the bus from its original position and has blended it into its new position.

The move isn't always 100% depending on the complexity and quality of your original image, so you may need to use the spot healing tool or the clone tool to touch up and repair the area.

Clone Stamp Tool

Sometimes it is necessary to remove an object from a photograph. We can do this with the Clone Stamp tool.

Open the **brightonlight.jpg** image.

In this photo I want to get rid of the street sign in the image. It just ruins the shot. To do this use the clone stamp.

Change the size of your brush in the options bar until it's about the size of the sign below.

Hold down ALT or OPTION on your keyboard and click an area close to the sign. This is the area we want to clone.

Try to sample as close to the spot you are going to remove as possible.

Paint over the sign a click at a time until the sign disappears.

Be patient and do it one click at a time as shown below. You'll notice as you move down the pole, the selected area moves parallel with it.

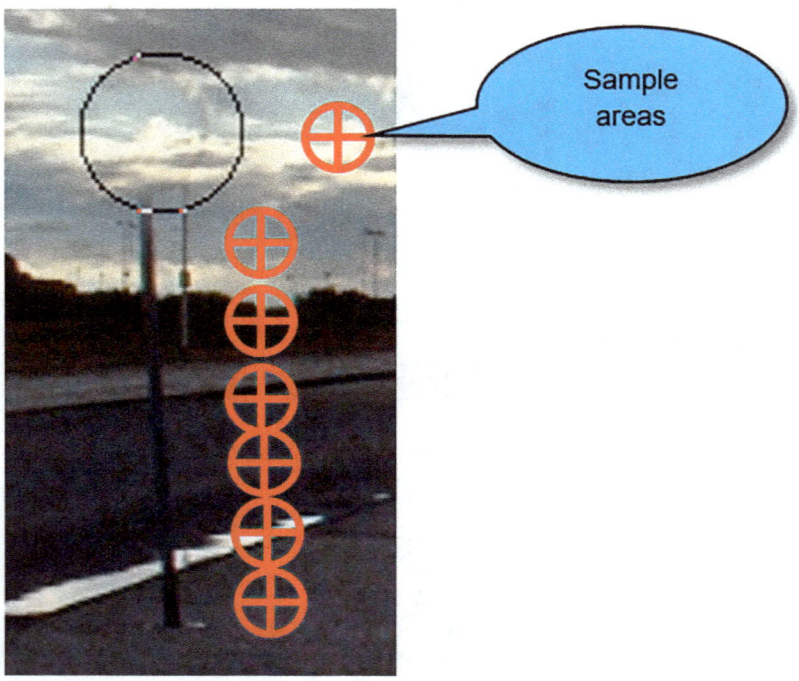

Challenge: Do the same with the sign's pole, this is a bit trickier as you have to clone the intricate details of the road.

Use the same technique as above do a small edge next to the pole and clone.

Magnetic Lasso Tool

This tool is useful if you want to select an object in an image and not the background. We can do this with the magnetic lasso.

Open the **daffodils.jpg** image.

Use the magnetic lasso to select the daffodils in the photo.

Now trace around the daffodils with the lasso, you will find that it will magnetically stick to the edge of the yellow flower. If it doesn't then click your mouse to manually add a point.

You can now copy and paste this. Go to edit menu -> copy, then edit menu -> paste.

Quick Selection Tool

Sometimes it is necessary to remove an object from an image. This is useful if you want the object and not the background. We can do this quickly the quick selection tool.

Open the **daffodils.jpg** image.

Use the quick selection tool to select the daffodils in the photo by clicking and dragging your mouse over the daffodils in the photo.

To remove any section selected that you don't want. Hold down alt/ option and click on that area to remove it from the selection

Magic Wand

The magic wand tool, selects areas of similar tone and colour.

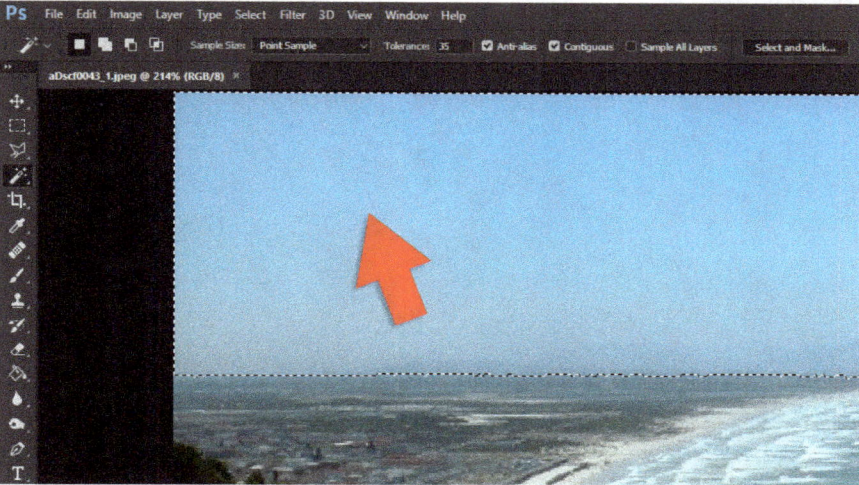

You can change the tolerance level in the options bar. The tolerance level is the difference in tone and colour a pixel is from the next.

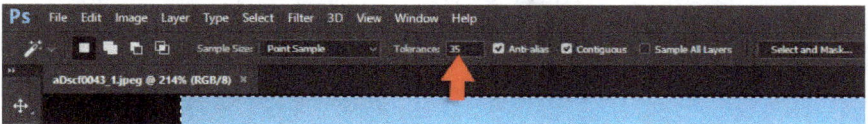

For example if the tolerance level is set to 35, magic wand will select any pixels that are the same colour as the colour you clicked on, plus any pixels up to 35 shades darker and 35 shades brighter.

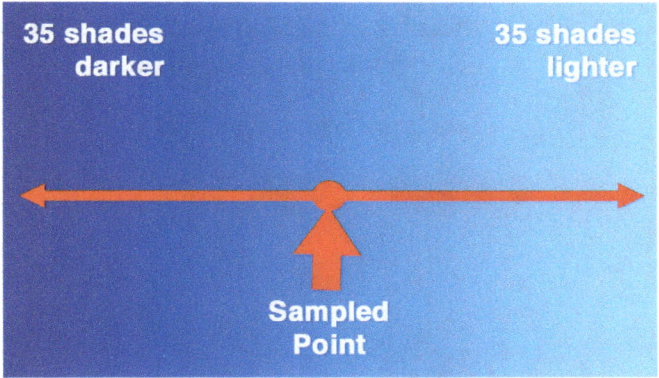

4 Using Layers

When you first open a photo, there is generally only a background layer.

This is where Photoshop really shows its power; the layers concept.

Layers allow you to build up complex designs using a layer to contain individual elements or objects that makes up parts of the whole design - like building blocks. This means that each element in the design can be created, edited and moved around quite easily without affecting everything else. This could be a title, photograph, shape and so on.

Lets begin by taking a look at a simple example.

The Layers Concept

We add layers to contain our effects, images and Photoshop objects. In the example below, I have a text layer and a photograph on another layer.

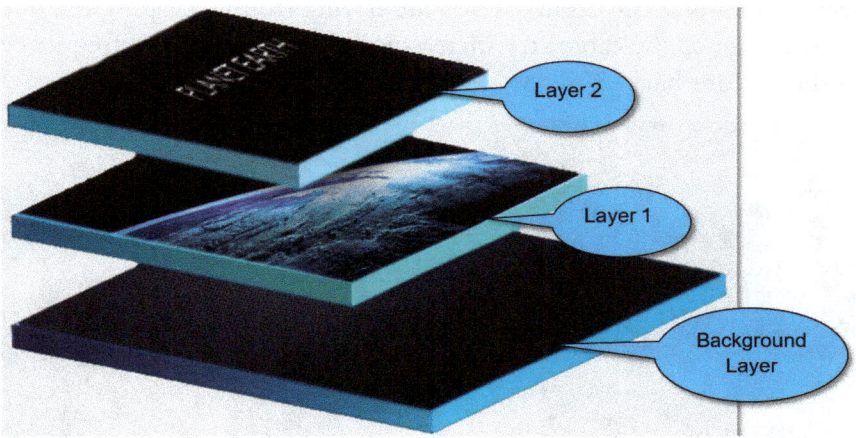

In the illustration above we can see a graphical representation of the Photoshop layers below in the layers panel.

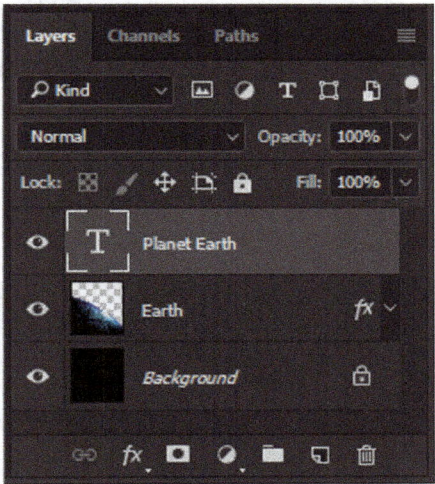

You can edit and arrange the objects on these layers independently; this could be some text, a shape or a photograph. In this way, you can build up multi layered projects and designs piece by piece.

Create an Image Collage

A collage is made up of two or more separate images. We'll use two images in this example; you can add more if you wish.

Open the **house.png** image. Using the magnetic lasso tool, make a selection around the cabin. If you are having trouble keeping the line on the edge of the cabin, try increasing the contrast or the frequency in the options bar.

When you close the loop, you will see the 'marching ants' around marking your selection.

Right click your mouse on the 'marching ants' selection, and from the popup menu select 'feather'. Set it to about 2px. This just softens the edge of the selected image.

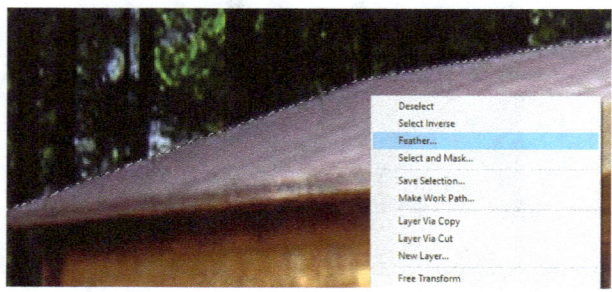

Go to edit menu > copy.

Now load up **lake.psd** then go to edit menu > paste. The cabin will appear on a new layer titled "Layer 1", in the layers panel.

With Layer 1 still highlighted in the layers panel, go to the edit menu > transform > scale. Drag the resize handles inwards as shown below.

Reduce the image to about 1/3 of its original size or until it fits nicely. Double click on the selection to execute the transform.

Using the move tool, place this image on the grass bank next to the water, so it looks like it's next to the river.

A challenge for you. Notice in the windows on the cabin door, you can see some of the original image. See if you can remove it to show the scene of the lake through the window.

Selection & Free Transform

Using the transform & scale tools, it is possible to resize and move objects, shapes or images on a particular layer.

Open the file **moon.png.**

Using the marquee tool select the moon.

Copy this selection by going to edit menu > copy.

Open up the **planetearth.psd** file.

Go to edit menu > paste. Make sure the image you just pasted is behind the earth. Go over to your layers panel and drag 'Layer 1' below the 'Earth' layer.

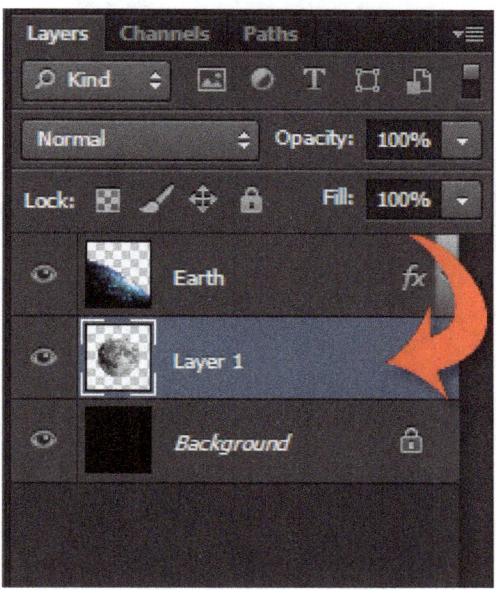

Chapter 4: Using Layers

Make sure 'layer 1' is selected in the layers panel.

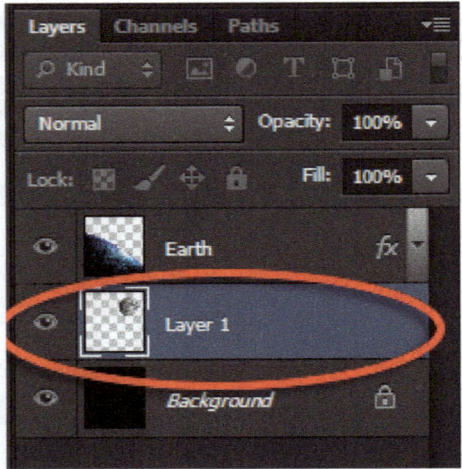

Go to edit menu > transform > scale.

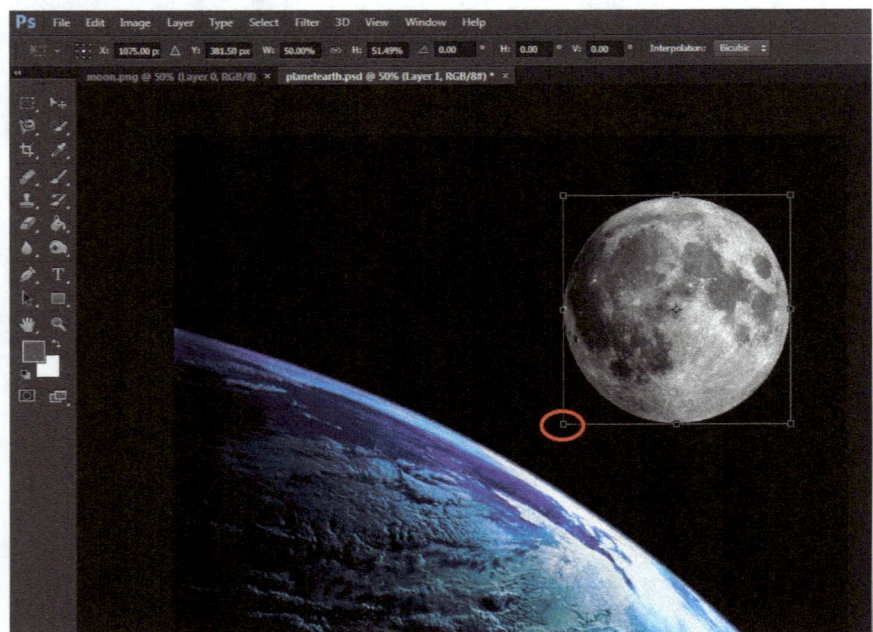

Drag the selectors, circled above, so that the moon seems smaller than the earth. When you're satisfied, double click on the moon image to execute the scale.

Layer Styles

Carrying on from the last section, if not, open the file **planetearth.psd**

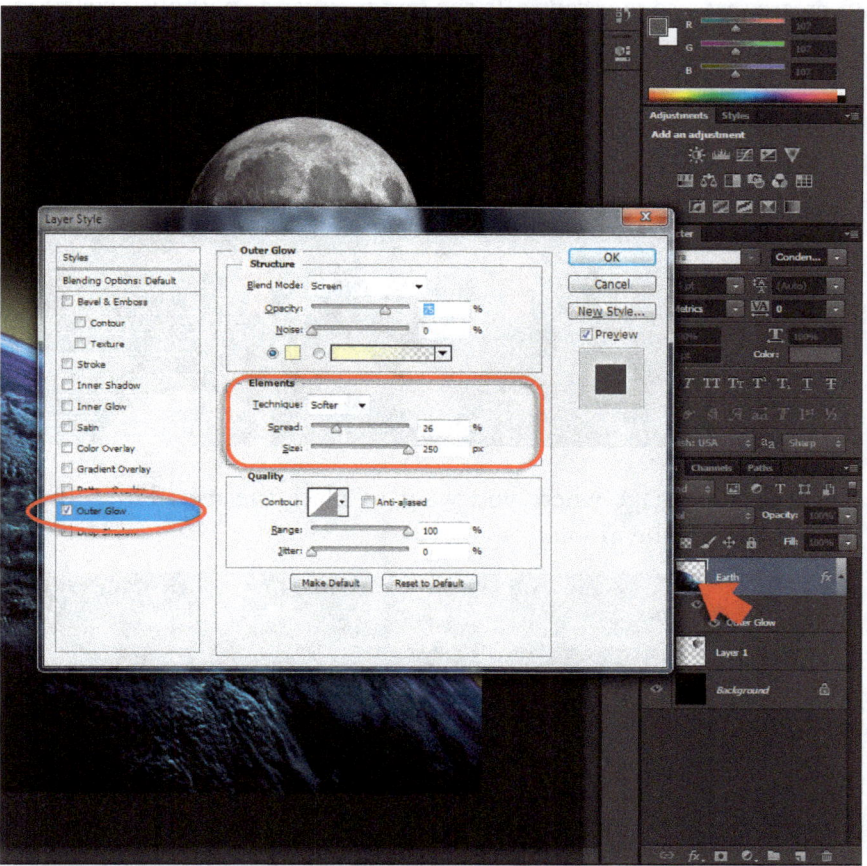

Double click on the earth layer in the layers panel to bring up layer style dialog box.

Click 'outer glow'.

Change the spread to a value of 26% and the size to a value of 250 px.

Click ok when you're done.

Effect not showing up? Right click on the effect in the layers panel and make sure 'show all effects' is selected.

Add Text

Let's use some text to title our image. Photoshop uses vector mapping to create text - so you can scale the text to any size without pixelation.

Carrying on from the last section, if not, open **planetearth.psd**

Select the text tool from your toolbox. Select a nice font, size and colour (eg #3d81ff) in the options bar shown below.

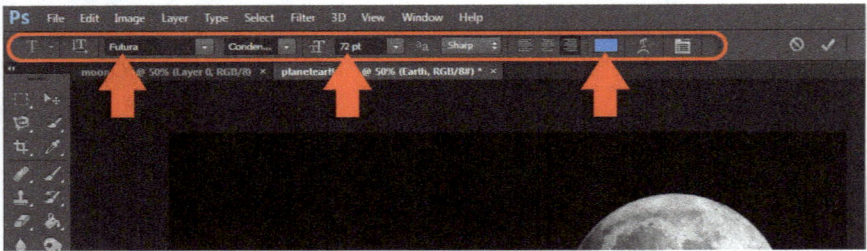

Click on the image where you want to place the text. I'm going to 'write' it across the moon.

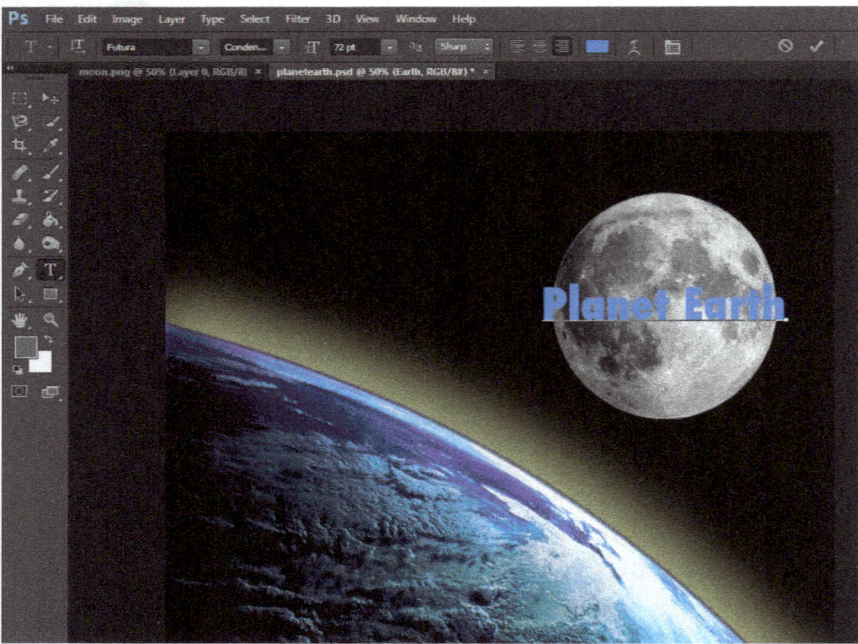

Type in a title. My title in this example is 'planet earth'.

Double click on the text layer you just created in the layers panel to bring up the layer style dialog box. Select 'bevel and emboss'.

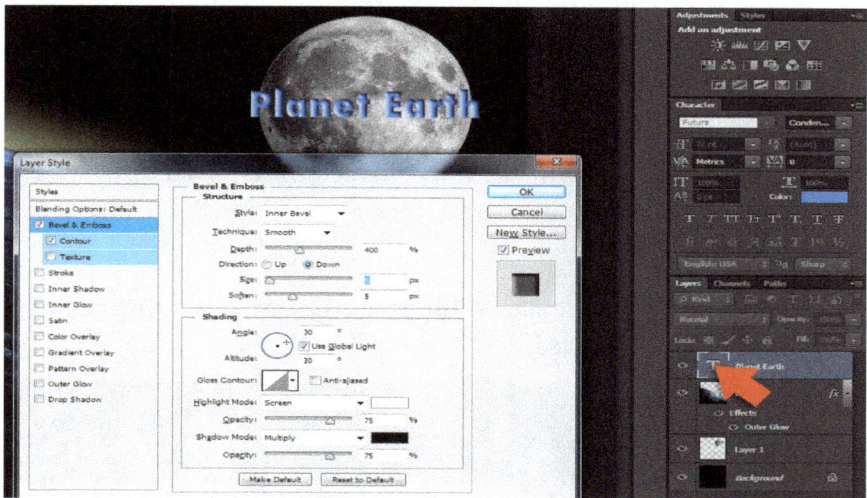

Experiment with the 'structure' and 'shading' settings and see how it affects the text. Click OK when you're happy.

Try experimenting with different effects. How about a nice outer glow?

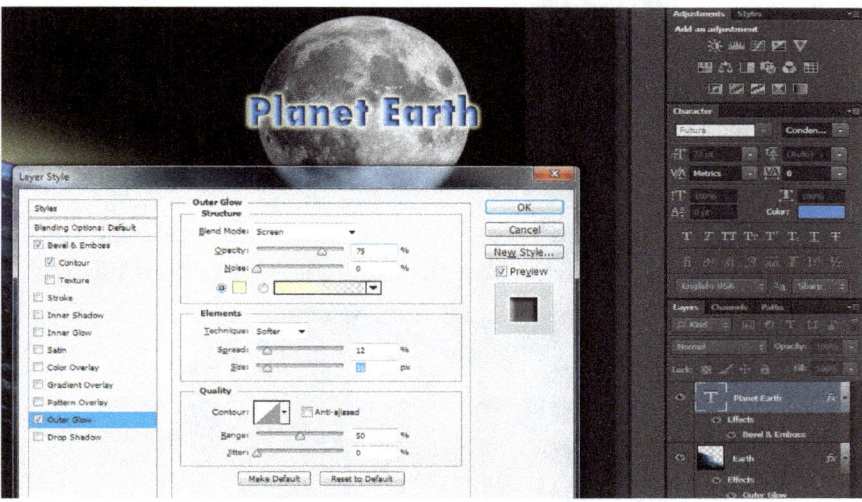

Now we can move this text to wherever we want. From the toolbox select the Move Tool. To adjust the position of this text, place the Move Tool on your text, click and drag it to the correct location.

Smart Objects

When you drag and drop an photograph or object into a Photoshop image, the object is pasted as a new layer and adopts the characteristics of the Photoshop image.

If you paste it in as a smart object, you can edit and build the object as an independent image with its own characteristics, layers, effects and so on. A smart object could be another Photoshop (PSD) image or a design from Illustrator.

To embed a Photoshop image or Illustrator design, select the file menu then click 'place embedded'.

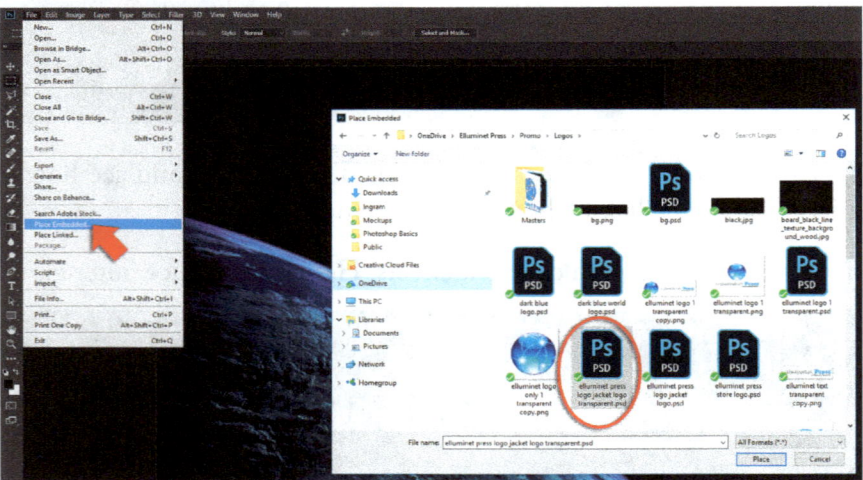

On your layers panel you'll see a small logo on the bottom right of the layer thumbnail. This means that the layer contains a smart object.

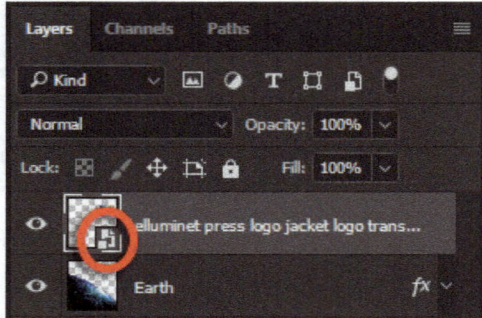

Now you can directly edit the smart object. To do this, double click on the layer thumbnail on your layers panel.

The smart object will open up in a new Photoshop window.

The layers panel will change to show the layers of the smart object you just opened. Here you can make independent changes and edit the object.

Once you are done, save and close the object file (file -> save) and it will automatically update.

Adjustment Layers

Adjustment layers alter all the layers below them, which makes them ideal for adjusting colour, contrast, brightness without altering individual layers.

You can find your basic adjustments on the adjustment panel. If the panel isn't open, go to the window menu and select 'adjustments'.

The adjustments available are shown below.

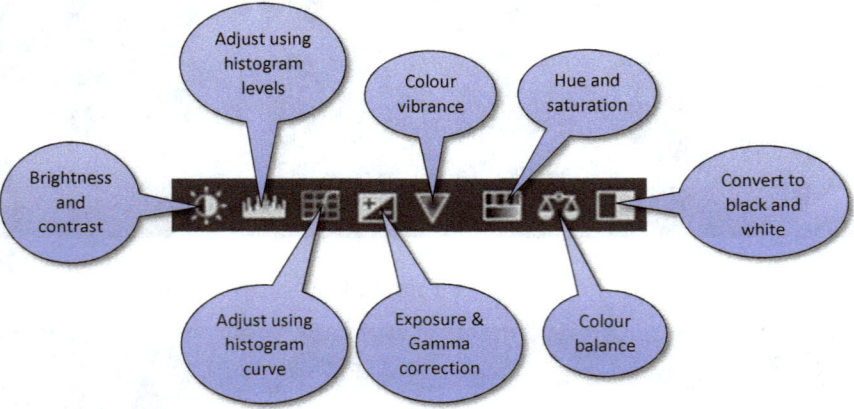

A few more advanced adjustments you can perform.

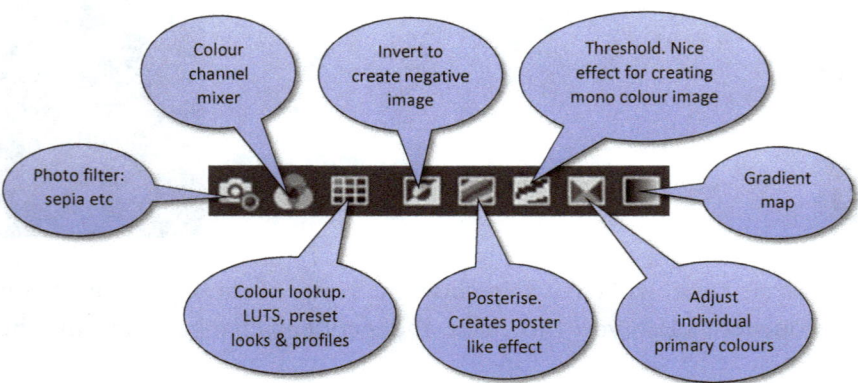

To apply any of these adjustments, click on the icon.

For this example, open **windowpasted.psd**. Notice that this project has multiple layers. Say I wanted to adjust the whole brightness or contrast of the whole image. If I attempt to use the adjustments on the image menu, the adjustment is only applied to the selected layer.

To apply an adjustment layer, select the top layer of your project. Remember the adjustment layer affects all layers underneath it.

From the adjustment panel, select the 'brightness' icon. Notice an adjustment layer has been added in the layers panel

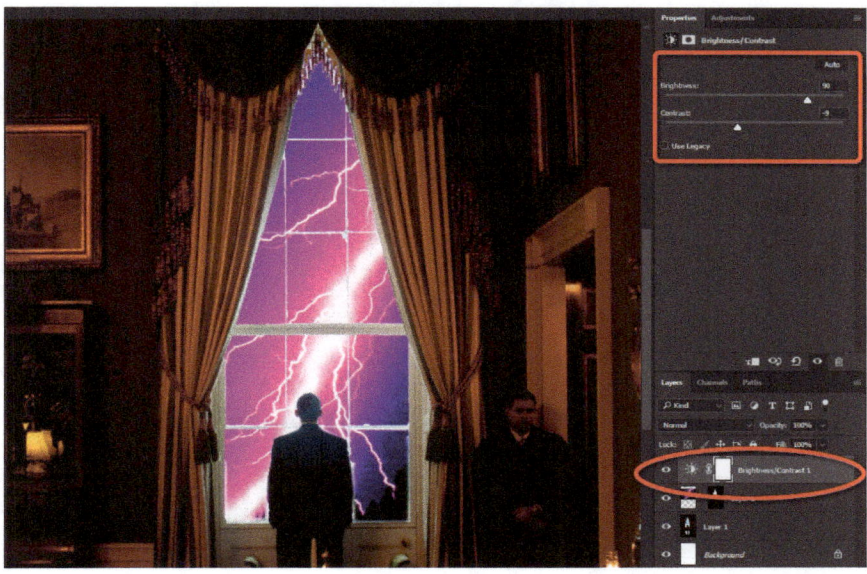

Some controls will appear in the properties panel. For this particular adjustment layer, we have brightness and contrast sliders. Move these until you have the desired brightness. Try applying some of the other adjustment layers see what they do.

Auto-align Layers

This is a great feature if you have multiple shots of the same scene you want to blend together.

A common example is a group shot at a wedding; not everyone is looking at the camera, some have their eyes closed because they blinked, or you have a number of different shots taken one after the other and you want to combine the best ones to create a new image, and so on. This only works with layers that have similar contents.

For this to work, your images need to be taken from the same perspective - the same position. Photoshop can't align the images if they're very different or taken from different angles. Try it, see what happens.

Open the file **one.jpg** from the auto align folder in the accompanying resources.

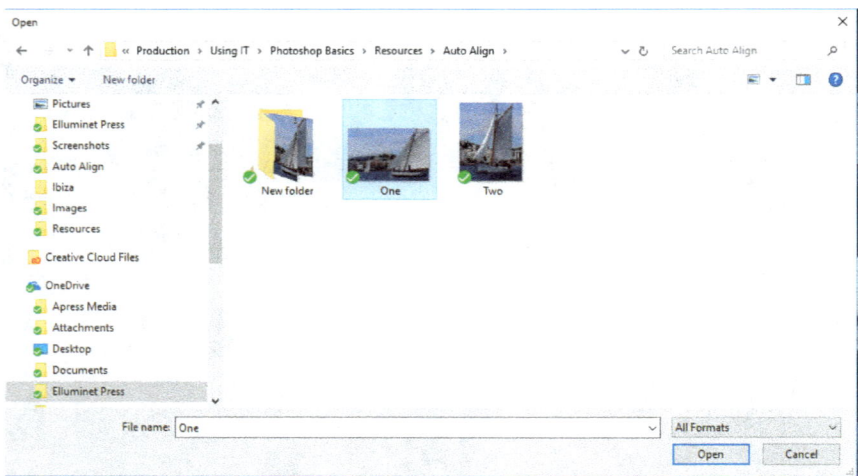

Open your file explorer or finder and navigate to the auto align folder, then drag and drop **two.jpg** on top of the open image. The image you just imported will be added as another layer.

Notice how the layers don't match and it would make a nice image if these two shots were combined.

To auto align the layers, first make sure all your layers are rasterized. If not right click on the layer name in the layers panel and select 'rasterize layer' from the popup menu.

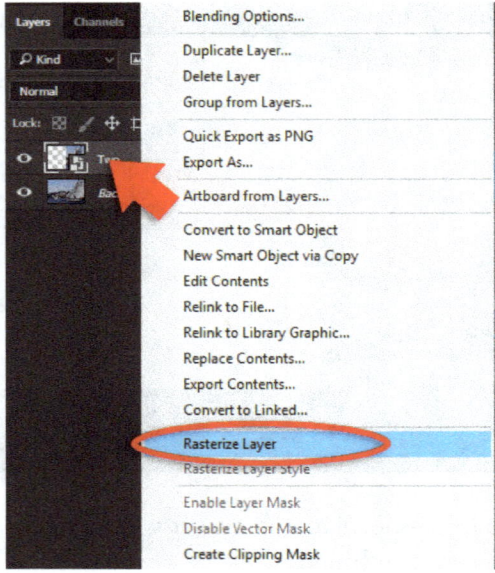

Next select both layers. Hold down control or command and click each layer.

From the edit menu, select 'auto align layers'. Select 'auto' from the dialog box, then click ok.

Photoshop will analyze the layers and attempt to align them together.

You might need to crop the image to remove any edges.

You can see it has created a much nicer composition than the original.

5 Special Effects

Photoshop has a large number of filters that you can apply to your images and give them a special look or characteristic.

Filters range from those that apply a particular painting effect to those that imitate different camera settings.

Filters

Photoshop has a large number of filters that allow you to add effects to your images.

- Sharpen filter (which helps sharpen up the edges of a slightly blurry image)
- Blur Effects (which can be used to create soft out of focus areas on an image)
- Lighting Effects
- Artistic Effects

You can find all your filters on the filters menu.

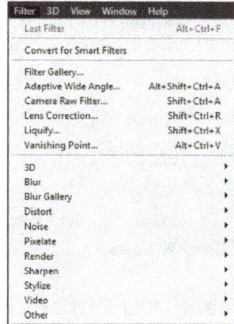

You can also browse through them in the filters gallery.

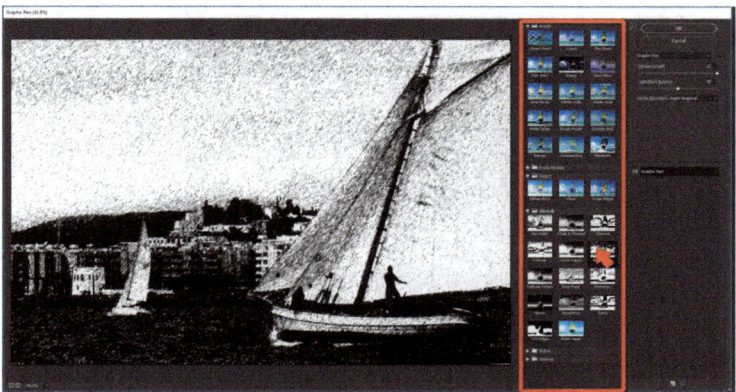

Here you can browse through the filters, circled in red above, and view the effects on your image.

Radial Blur

Open the **carwindow.jpg** image. Select 'radial blur'. The entire image now looks like the car is moving really fast.

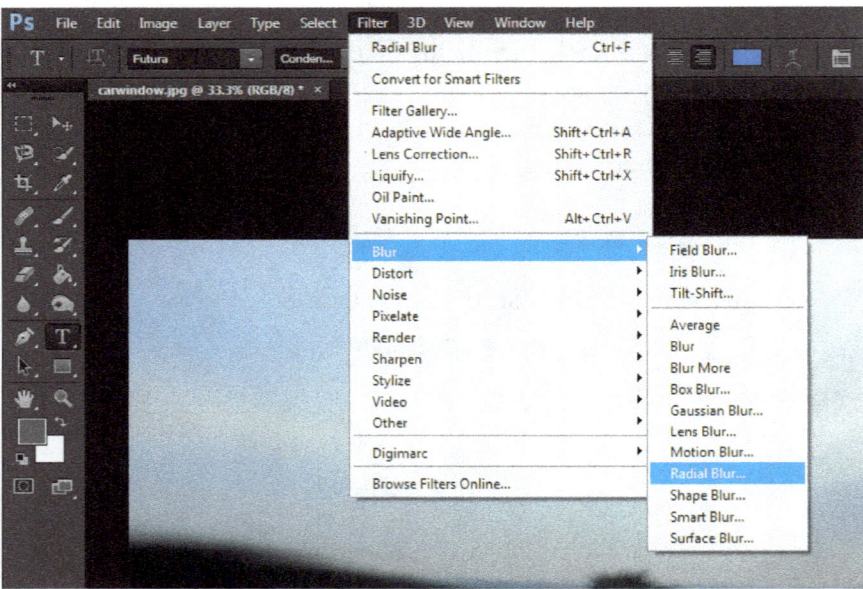

In the dialog box that appears, you can adjust the amount of blur, the method: make it look like it's spinning or moving fast, and the quality.

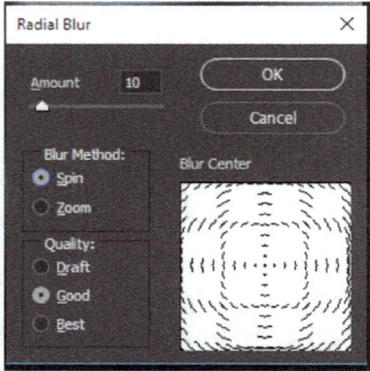

Experiment with applying different amounts of radial blur using the slider at the top of the window. Try the two different methods of blur: spin & zoom, and see what effect they have on the image.

Stylize Filters

Stylize filters allow you to create a painted or impressionistic effect on your images. Select 'stylize' from the 'filter' menu.

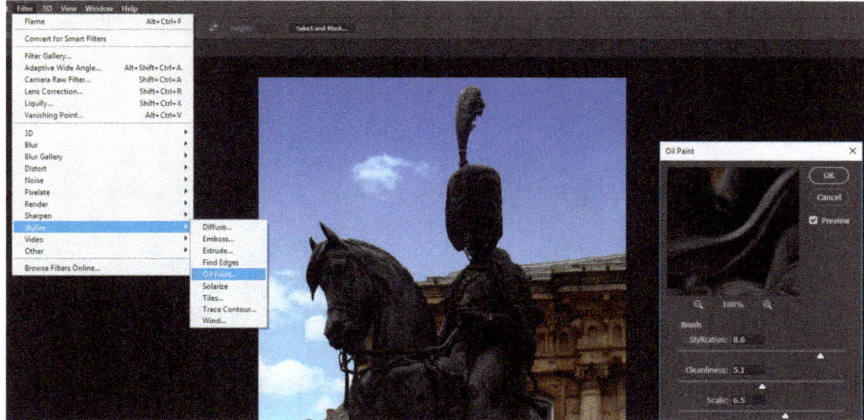

From the slide out, select 'oil paint'. Turn your image into a vangogh. Click the check box next to 'preview' then use the sliders on the right hand side of the dialog box for stylization and detail of the oil pant effect. Try each one and see what it does to the image.

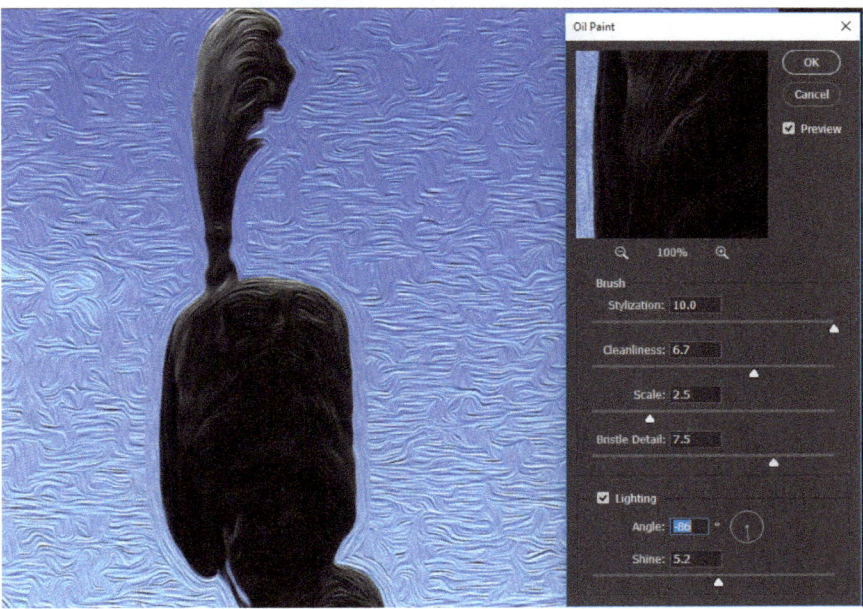

Filter Gallery

The filter gallery is useful for trying different filters and see the immediate result in the preview window. This helps you experiment and try out new ideas without applying the filter each time.

Open the file **statue.jpg** from the resources folder.

Open the filter gallery. Go to the filter menu and select 'filter gallery'.

When you open the filter gallery you'll see a preview of the currently open image on the left and a list of filters and controls on the right hand side.

To apply the filters, open up the folders and select a thumbnail. In this example, I'm going to apply a graphic pen filter to my image.

Now, over on the right hand side of the screen, you'll see some controls that allow you to adjust the effect of the filter. These tend to change depending on which filter you've selected. In this case, you can adjust the length of each pen stroke, the amount of light and dark strokes, and the direction of the pen stroke.

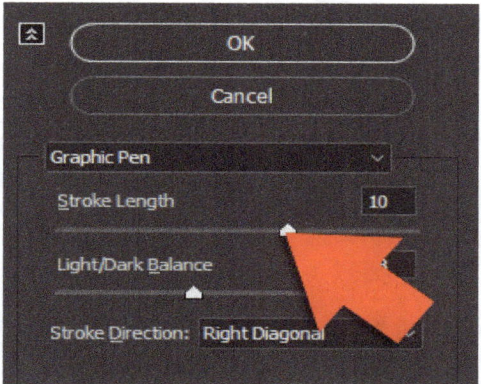

Try adjusting these using the sliders and see what happens to the image. Click OK when you're happy to apply the filter to the image. Here's and example.

Try some of the other filters and see what happens.

Lighting Effects

Lighting effects in Photoshop requires 3D functionality - so you will need a graphics card, and an OS that supports OpenGL and 3D functionality.

To check go to preferences (under the Photoshop menu on Mac, under the Edit menu on Windows) > Performance & 3D.

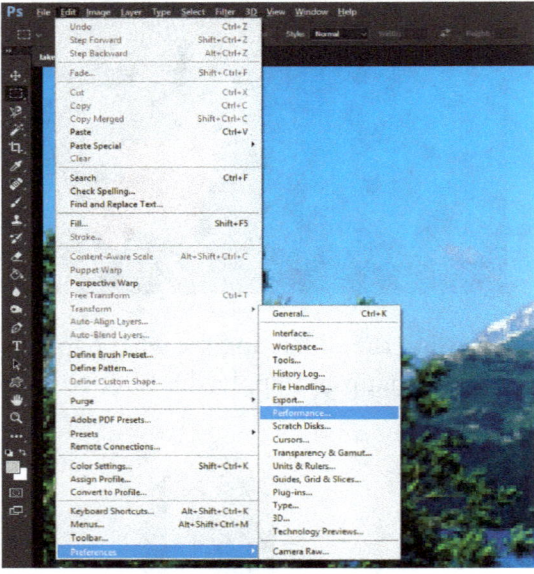

Is "Use Graphics Processor" checked, or is it greyed out? If so, you will have to use the classic effects.

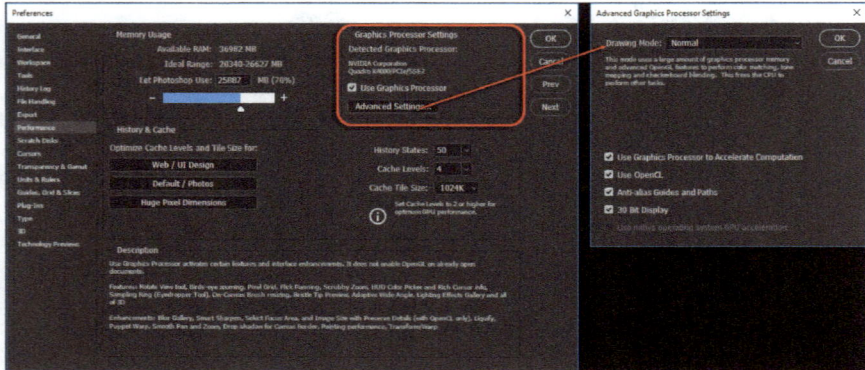

Lighting effects only supports 8 bit/channel RGB images. Change this using the 'image' menu. Select the settings from the 'mode' slide out.

Open **house.png** image and from the filter menu click 'render' then 'lighting effects'.

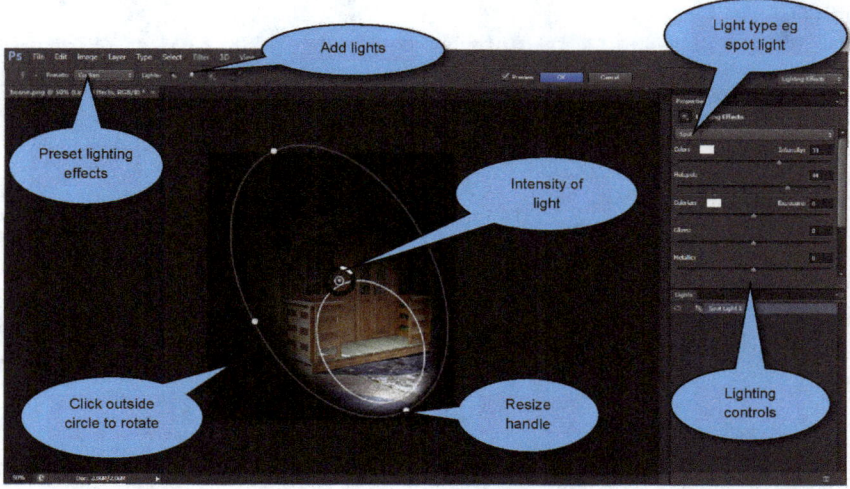

From the lighting effects panel on the right hand side you can choose a number of different types of lights, colour and adjust the intensity, direction and focus.

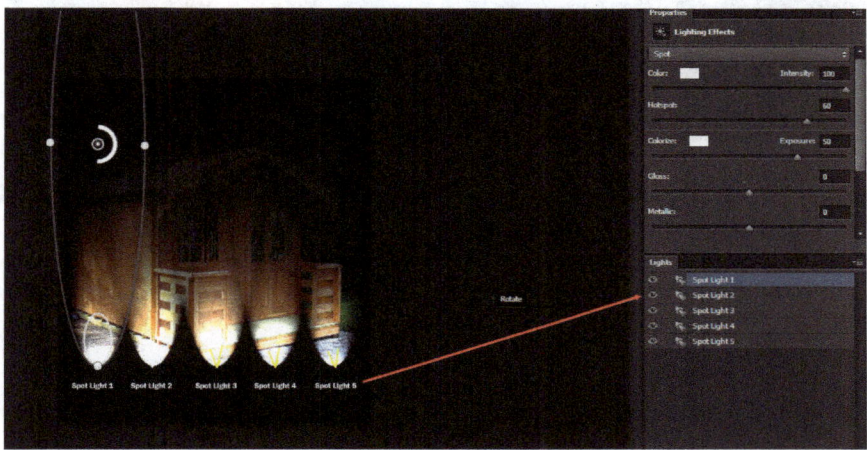

Drag the lights into position and drag the resize handles to resize and rotate them.

Chapter 5: Special Effects

Try experimenting with different light settings.

Here I added two spot lights, changed the colour and intensity, and arranged them outside my house.

Combining Photos

You can use the selection tools and the 'past into' command to create interesting special effects. In the example below, lightening will be added behind the windows in a second photo to give the effect that the there is a storm inside a building.

Open the **lightning.jpg** image.

Use the Brightness/Contrast menu to adjust the image if desired - for this particular image, I'm not going to make any brightness adjustments.

Select the whole image with the marquee selection tool from your toolbox.

Use the copy command from the edit menu, to copy the selection to the clipboard.

Chapter 5: Special Effects

Open the **window.psd** image.

Select the rectangular marquee tool, start in one of the square window panes and select the interior of the pane. You might want to zoom right into your picture to do this. Make sure that the style of the marquee tool is set to 'normal' in the options bar.

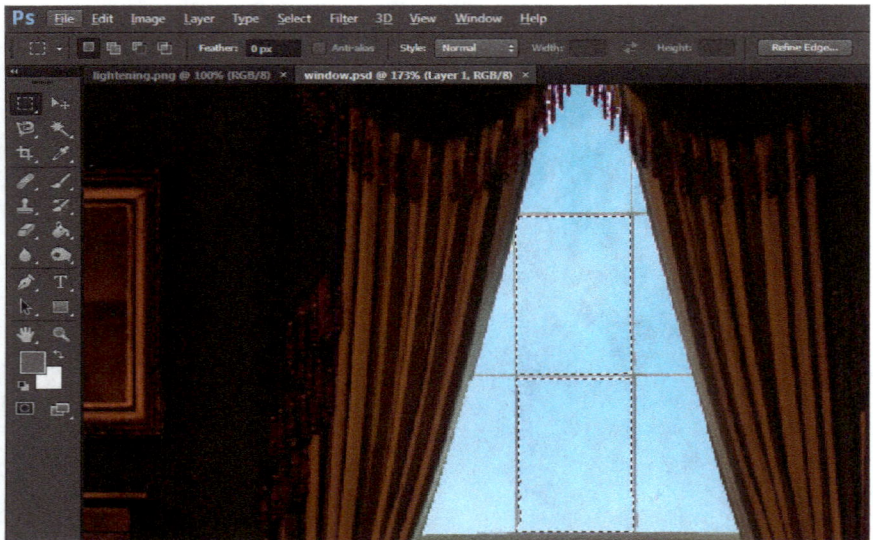

Hold down the shift key and select the other full square window panes.

Now still holding the shift key, select the magnetic lasso tool to select the triangular shapes at the top of the window - trace around the inner edges of the window panes. Do this until all the sky blue is selected.

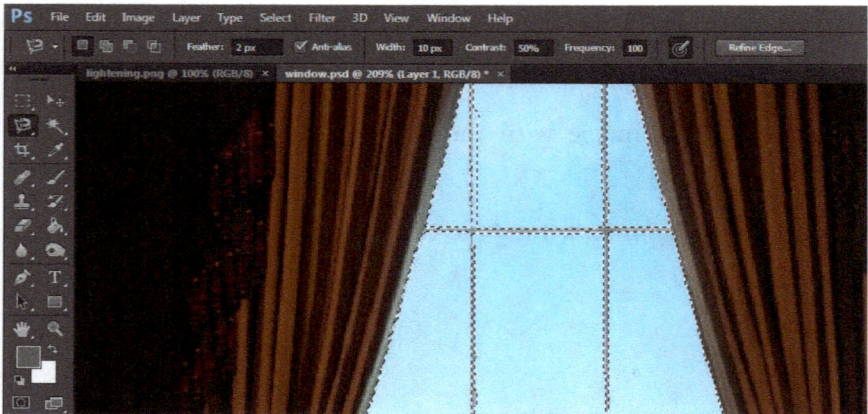

Once all the shapes are selected, go to...

Edit menu -> paste special -> select the 'paste into'.

This will paste into the selection, the lightning picture we copied earlier. The 'paste into' command pastes the lightning picture we copied behind the window panes we cut out.

Now select the 'move tool' from your toolbox, and move the lightning picture around until you like the effect in the windows. The window picture has effectively become a mask for the lightning picture which lies behind it.

A challenge for you. You might also notice there is a reflection on the table, see if you can create a reflection of the lightning storm on the table to match the one seen through the window.

6 3D Effects

3D functionality requires a capable graphics card, and an OS that can support OpenGL, OpenCL and 3D features.

A good Nvidia Quadro or GeForce graphics/video card is recommended for Adobe applications and will allow you to use all the advanced features in Photoshop.

You can find out what hardware you have if you go to Photoshop's preferences and select performance. On the top right of the dialog box, you'll see graphics processor details.

Creating 3D Objects

For this exercise open up **earthmap.jpg**

To start using 3D, you'll need to open up the 3D panel. Go to the window menu and select '3D'. A panel will open on the right hand side of your screen.

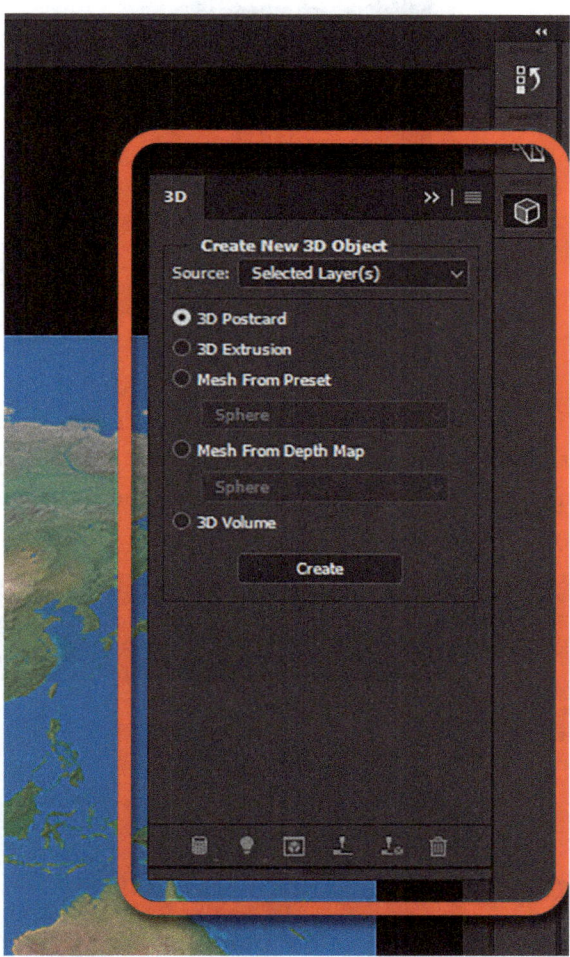

Here you'll be able to create 3D objects from layers, paths or objects.

3D Postcard

The easiest way to create 3D is by taking a layer and generating a 3D plane, or postcard. With the background layer set as your source, choose 3D Postcard from the 3D tab and Photoshop will create a 3D plane based on the pixels in your layer.

A postcard is also useful if you want to generate a plane to catch reflections, shadows, lighting, effects, etc. You can orient the plane perpendicular to your object and then merge the 3D objects together to a single layer.

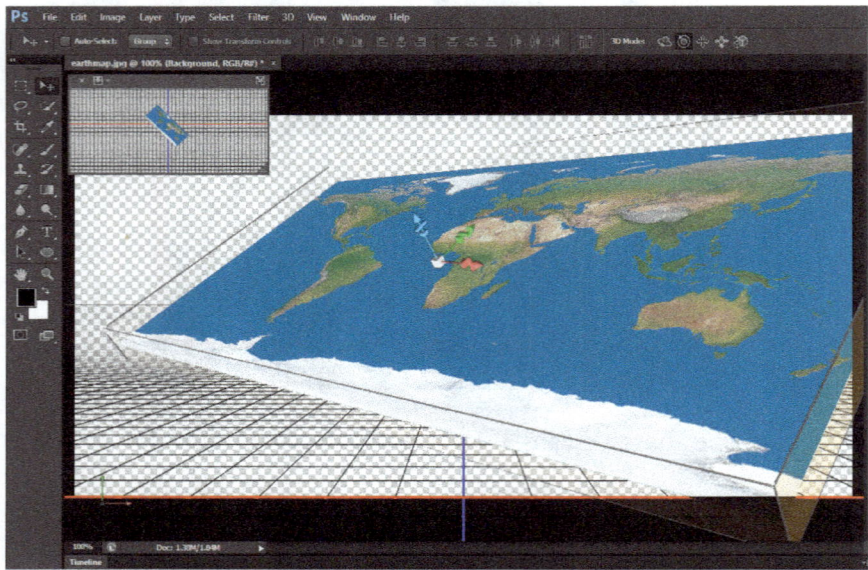

3D Extrusion

To create a 3D extrusion, select 'extrusion' from the 3D panel on the bottom right of your screen.

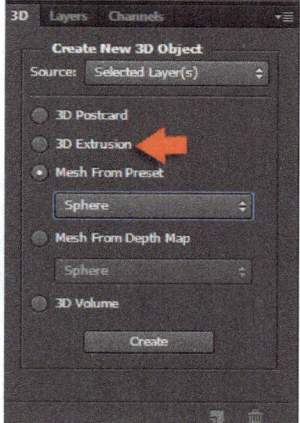

Add some text with the text tool, select 3D extrusion on the 3D tab on the layers panel.

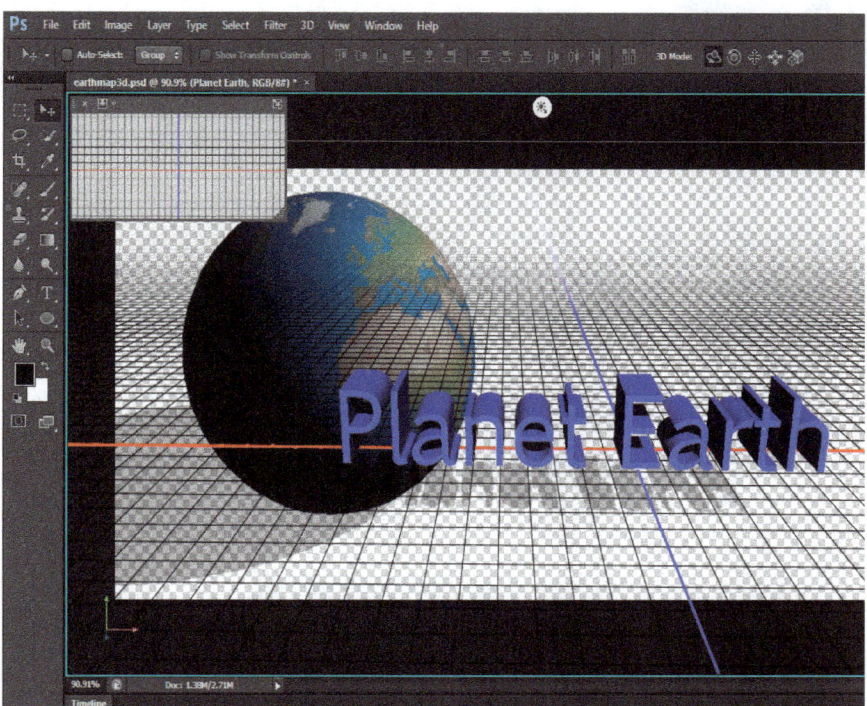

3D Shape from Preset

You can also take this layer and wrap it around any 3D shape, such as a sphere, cube, cylinder and so on.

Open **earthmap.jpg**

In this example, I am going to take the map of the earth and wrap it around a sphere.

From the 3D panel, click 'mesh from preset'. Then change the shape selection to 'sphere'.

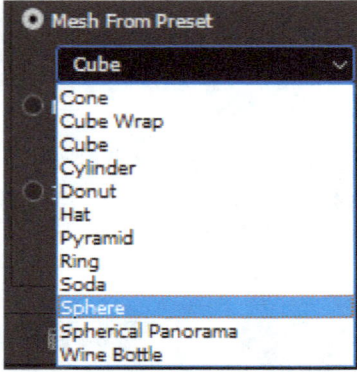

Click 'create' at the bottom of the 3D panel when you've done that.

Add some 3D Text

Select your text tool and type some text next to the 3D earth. Then hit hour 3D button to convert it to a 3D object.

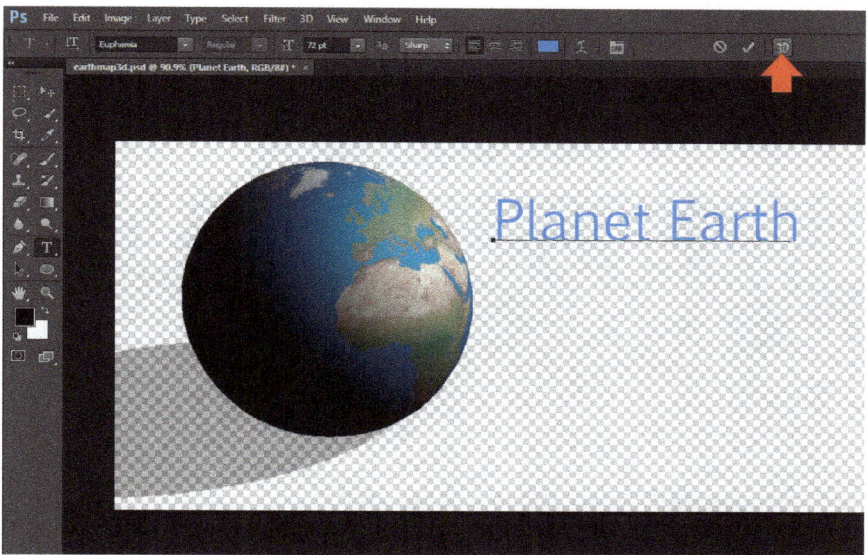

Click on the text object and using the 3D controls position your text accordingly so it looks good next to the planet.

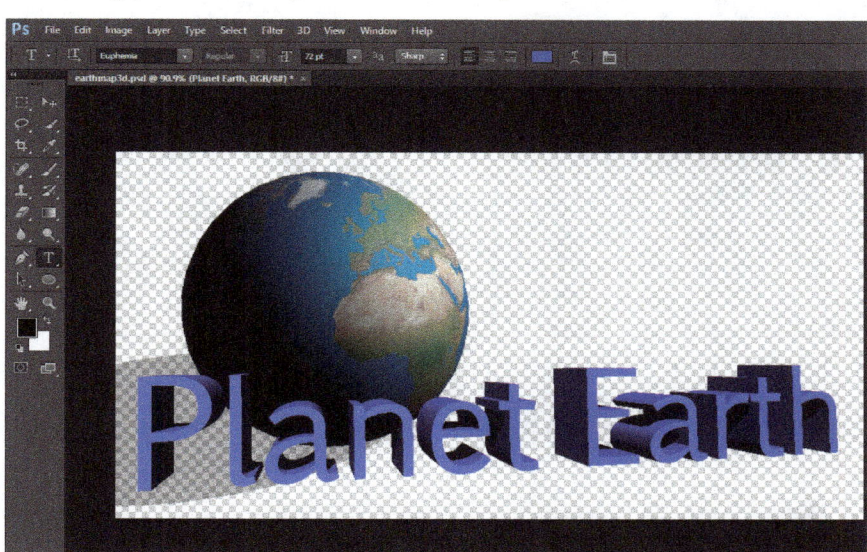

Navigating 3D

Lets take a brief look at the 3D controls for moving and sizing your 3D objects.

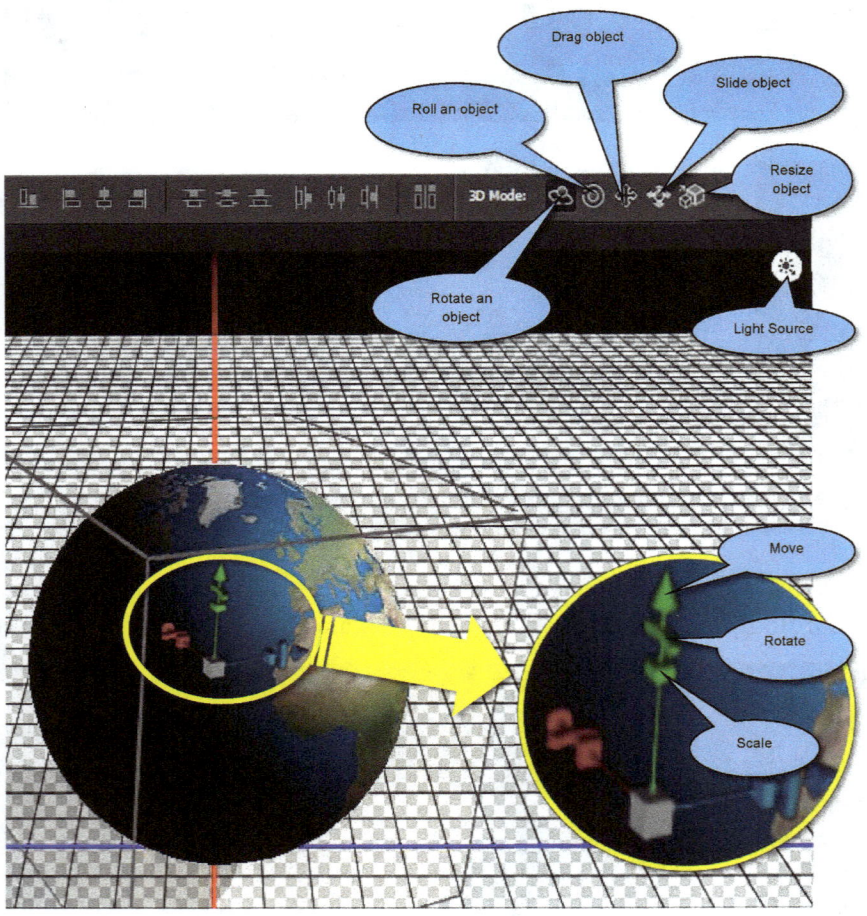

Each 3D object has a handle with 3 axis on it. These axis are for moving and manipulating the object in 3D space.

- Red is X-axis (left/right)

- Green is Y-axis (up/down)

- Blue is Z-axis (nearer/farther)

Moving Around your Object

You can move your view around in 3D space. Your view point is usually represented by a virtual camera and you can move this using the controls on the bottom left of your screen.

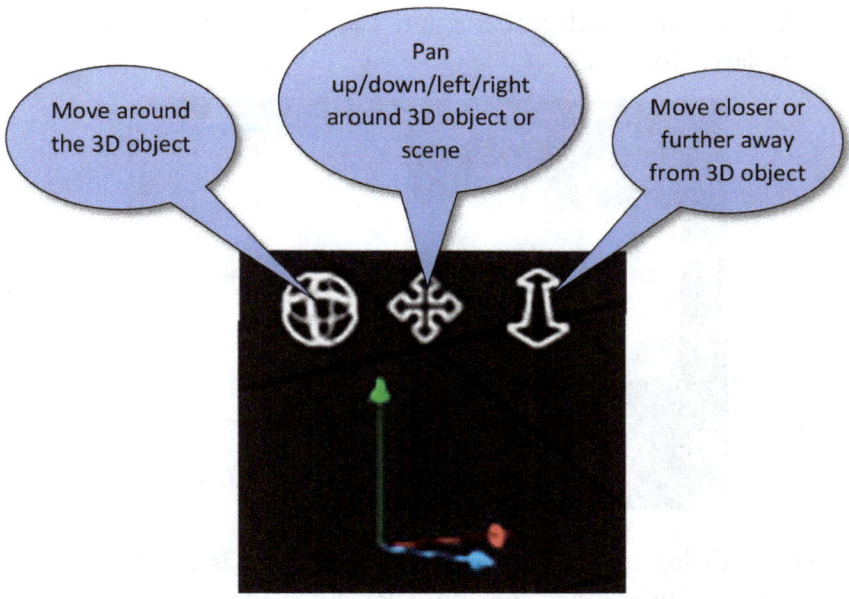

For this demonstration open the file **3D.psd** in the resources folder for this book.

First, select your move tool from the toolbox on the left hand side, then click on the object you want to have a look at. If you can't click on it, select the layer the object is on from the layers panel.

Click on the icon, then while holding the button down, move your mouse to adjust your view.

As an example, click and hold your mouse button on the first icon. Now while you're holding your mouse button down, move your mouse up, down, left, and right and see what happens.

Try the other two icons and see what they do.

Inserting 3D Models

You can insert 3D models created in 3Ds or any 3D modeling software. Many of these are available for download on the internet.

If you haven't already opened a new photoshop document, do that now. File -> New -> Select size eg A4. Then from the 3D menu, select 'new 3d layer from file'.

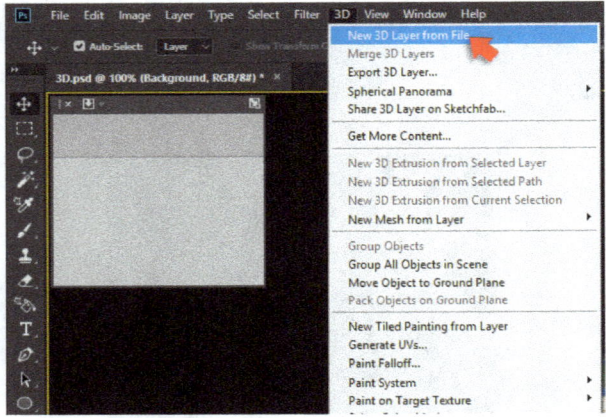

From the dialog box choose a 3D model. There is one included in the resources folder called **spaceshuttleorbiter.3ds** for you to use and experiment with.

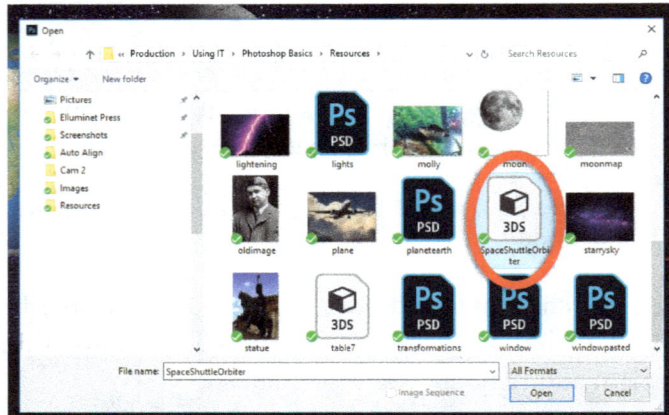

The model will be added as a new 3D layer which you can manipulate, resize and move into your scene.

Select the size of your scene; your environment. For most of the models, you can leave the settings at their default. Click OK.

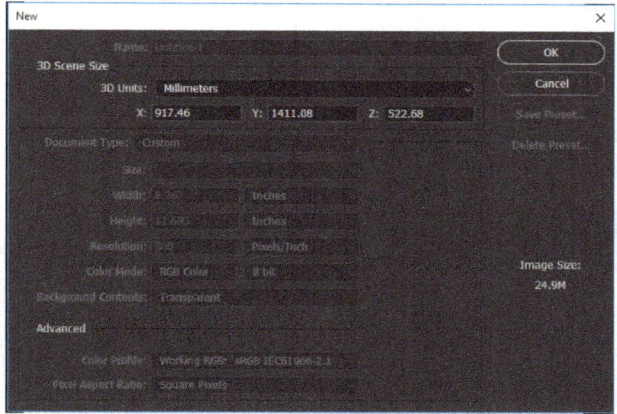

Select your move tool from the tool box on the top left and click on your model.

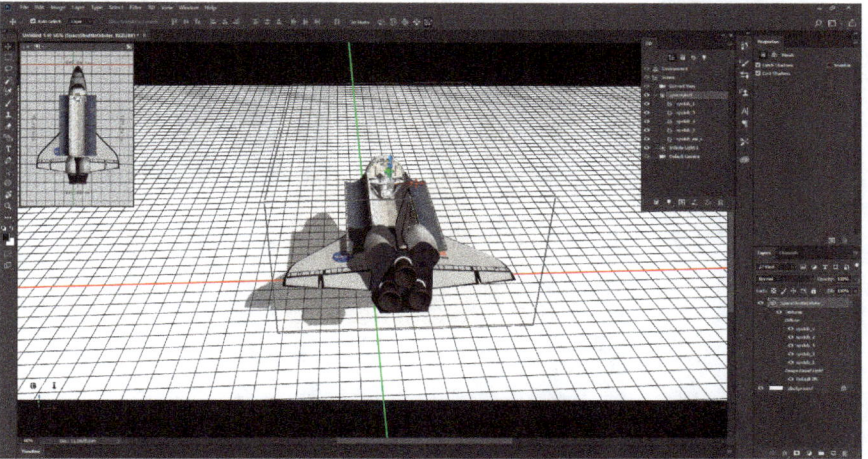

Use the navigation options on the bottom left of the screen to move around your model. Note this moves your point of view not the position of the model.

Build your Scene

You can build up a 3D scene using layers in a similar fashion to 2D projects we have looked at earlier. For this example open **3D earth. psd**.

We can insert a background. Open your file explorer or finder. Drag and drop **starrysky.jpg** into your project

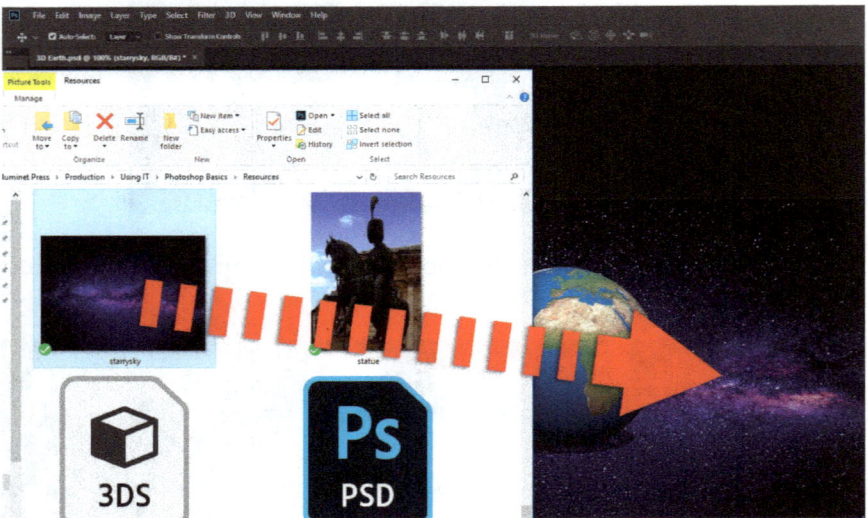

Move the starrysky layer below the earth layer - to put it behind.

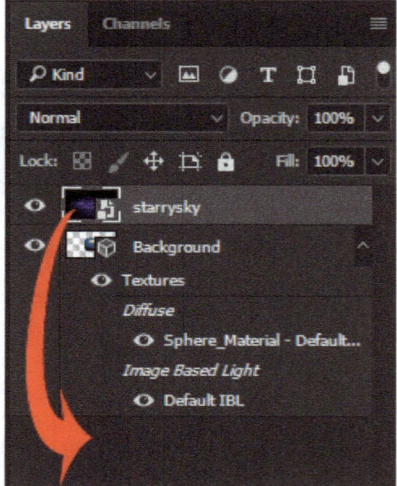

Now, open your file explorer or finder and drag and drop **moonmap. jpg** from the resources folder. Press enter on your keyboard to insert the layer.

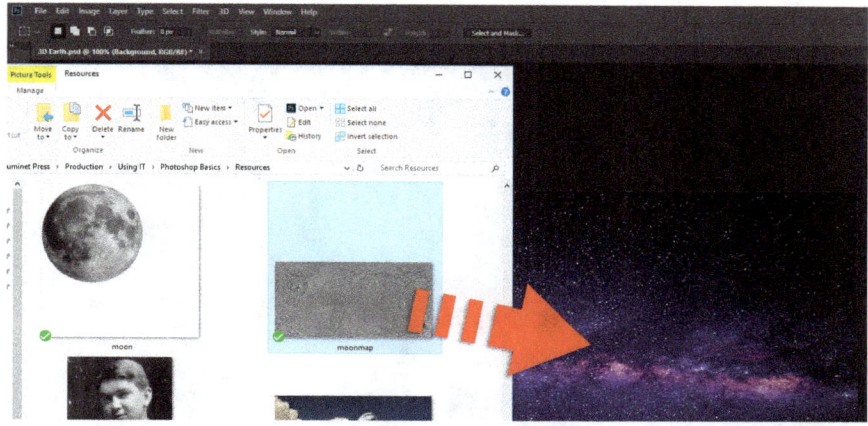

We need to create a 3D object from this layer, so we're going to map the image onto a sphere. From the 3D panel, select 'mesh from preset' and in the drop down select 'sphere'. Hit 'create'.

Select your move tool from the tool box on the left hand side. Click on an object, the moon for example. Use the 3D navigation to move the object in 3D space.

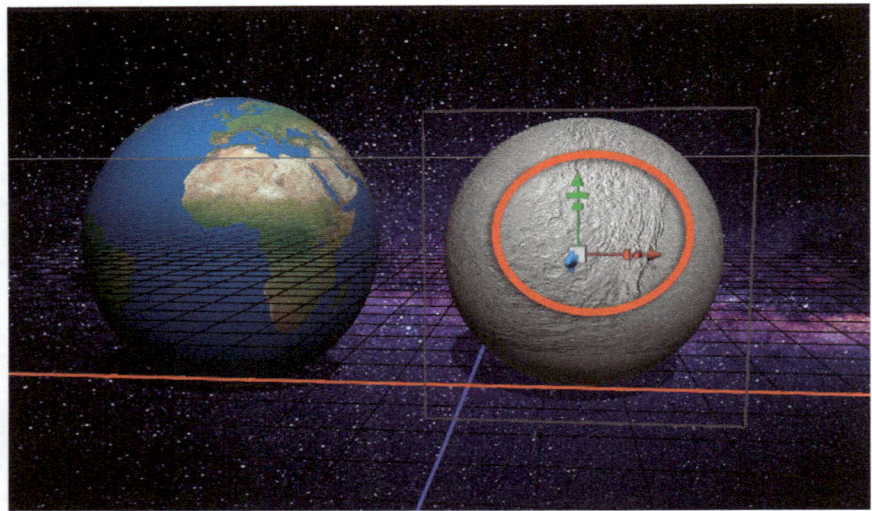

By default, Photoshop adds 3D objects as independent 3D layers. This means they don't interact, cast shadows onto each other and so on.

Notice each object in the 3D panel has its own light source and environment - you can adjust the light on each object.

In the example below, the light on the moon isn't casting a shadow on the earth object.

To get objects to interact, you have to merge the layers they're on. For this example, I am going to merge the earth and moon layers. So select both of these in the layers panel. Now go to the 3D menu and select 'merge 3D layers'.

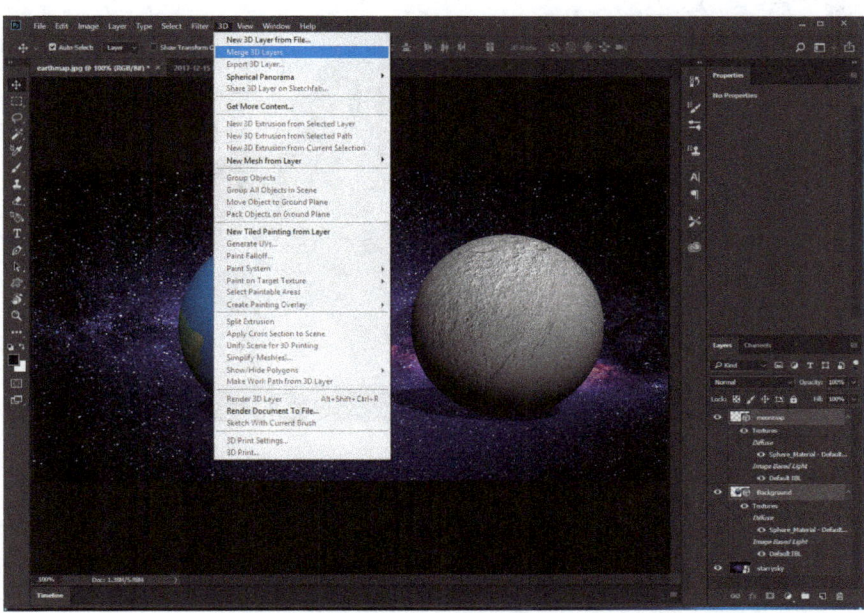

Notice now, there is a shadow on the earth cast by the moon object.

Both the objects now appear in the 3D panel.

Select the move tool from the tool box on the left hand side. In the 3D panel, select 'infinite light 1'. This is the light source for these objects.

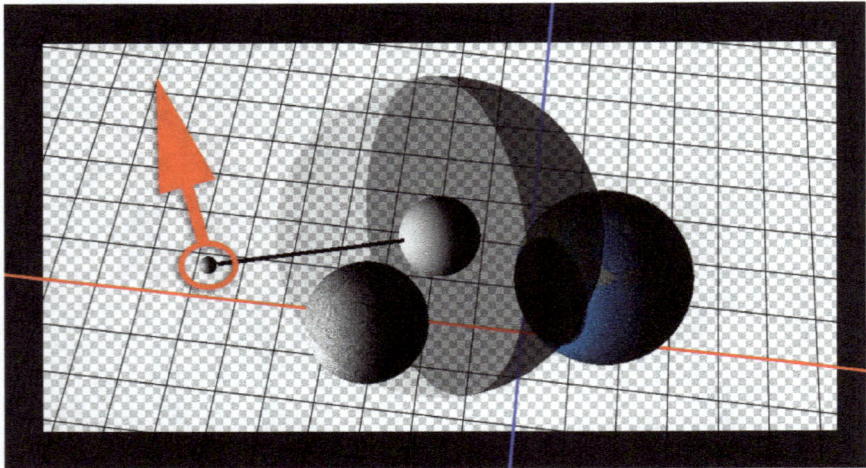

Grab the small ball on the end of the line and drag it around to reposition the light. You'll be able to see the shadows change depending on where you put the light.

You can add more lights. On your 3D panel, click the lightbulb icon on the bottom row.

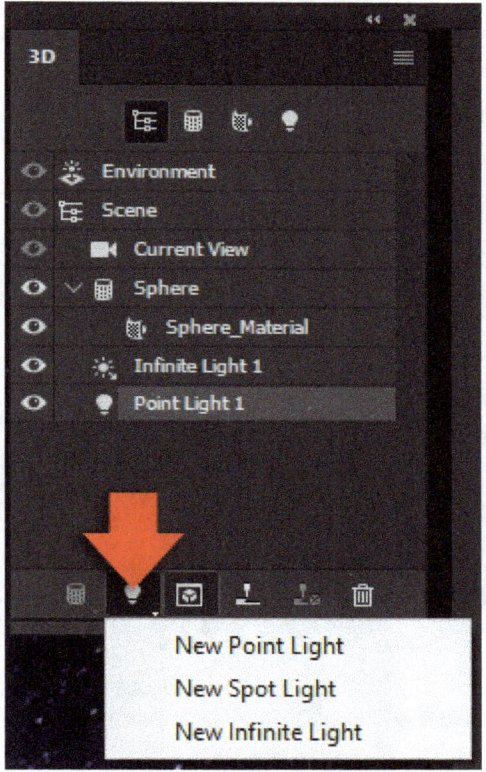

You can add three types of lights.

- A spot light provides a very direct source of light

- A point light emits light in all directions.

- An infinite light shines from one direction similar to sunlight.

Select a 'new spot light' from the drop down menu.

Select your move tool from the toolbox on the left hand side if you haven't already got it selected.

Click 'spot light' in your 3D panel. This is the light you just created.

On your screen, you'll see two cones emanating from the light source. This is to control the focus of your light beam. Click and drag the handles on the inner cone to adjust the centre of the beam and use the outer one to set the focus on a wide area or just a small area.

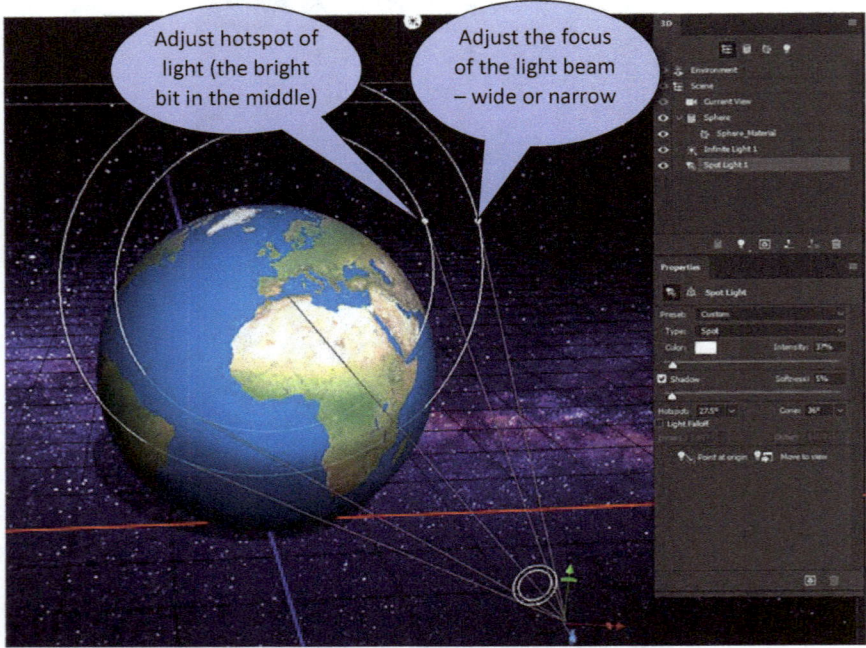

Use the standard 3D handles on the light to move and aim it in your scene

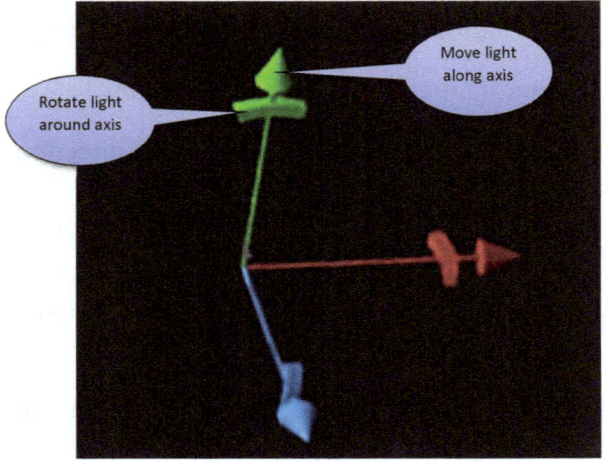

On the properties panel, you can adjust the intensity, type, colour, shadow effect, the size of the hotspot in the middle of the light (the bright bit) and the cone to focus the light or widen the light beam.

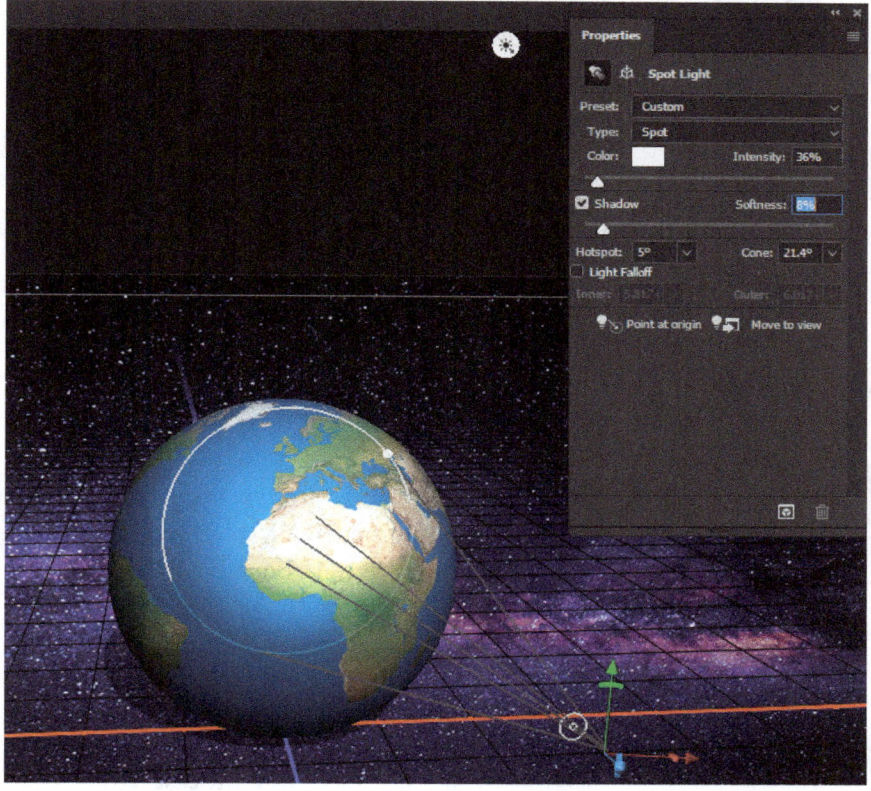

Experiment with some of these settings and see what happens.

7 Photoshop for Photography

For best results, it is always advisable to shoot your photographs in RAW format, rather than JPG. This allows a lot more flexibility when it comes to post production - adjusting brightness, shadows, contrast, colour and so on.

Think of RAW files along the same lines as a negative as was used in the old film days; or digital negative today. You process your RAW photos then save them out as JPG to use on the web, post on social media or some design project. This means you always have a copy of your original photograph you can go back to.

Import Photos

You can either import photos using Adobe Bridge or Lightroom. These are two separate Adobe applications and will not be covering these here, our focus is Photoshop.

In Adobe Bridge, click the file menu and select 'get photos from camera'. From the dialog box that appears click 'advanced dialog' on the bottom left.

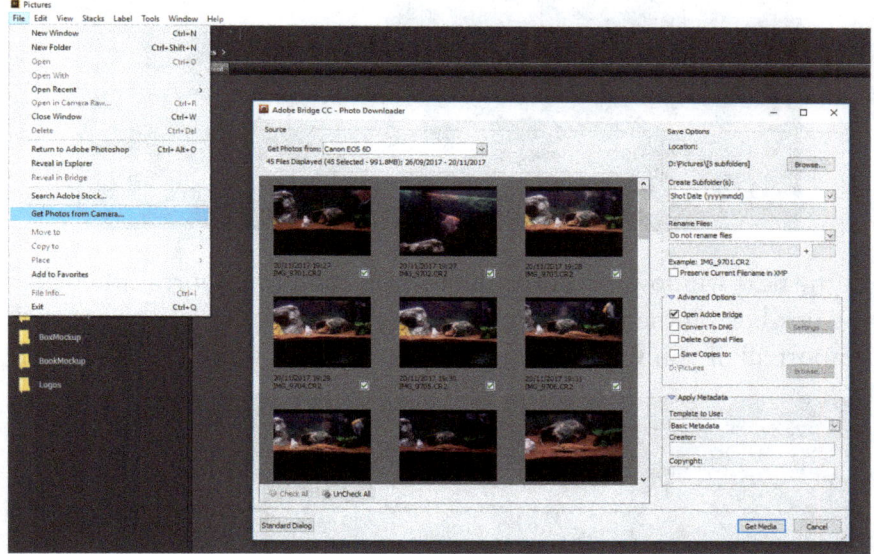

Click the tick box on the top left of each image you want to import.

On the right hand side, select 'browse'. This is the folder on your computer where you want Bridge to store all your photos. I usually select the 'pictures' directory.

Once you're done click 'Get Media' on the bottom right.

If you have Lightroom, connect your camera and hit 'import' on the bottom left of the screen.

In the next window, select the photos you want to import. Either click the tick box on the top left of each image you want to import, or click 'import all' if you want to import every photo on your camera.

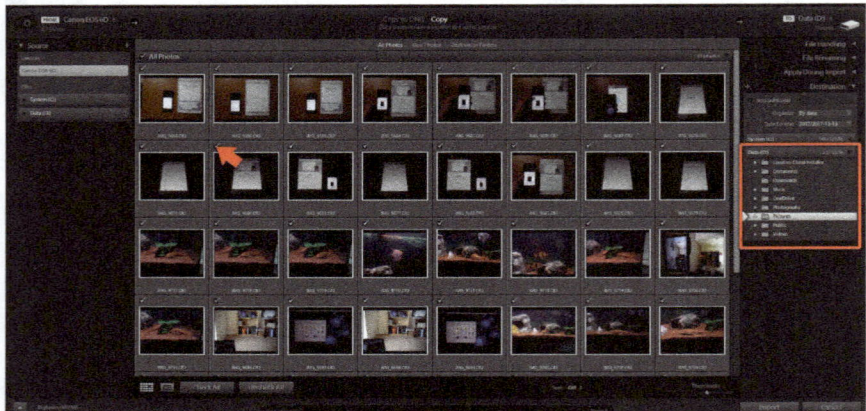

On the right hand side, select 'destination'. This is the folder on your computer where you want Lightroom to store all your photos. I usually select the 'pictures' directory. Once you're done click 'import' on the bottom right.

You can open any image in Photoshop from Lightroom. Right click on the image thumbnail, go down to 'edit in', then select 'Photoshop...'.

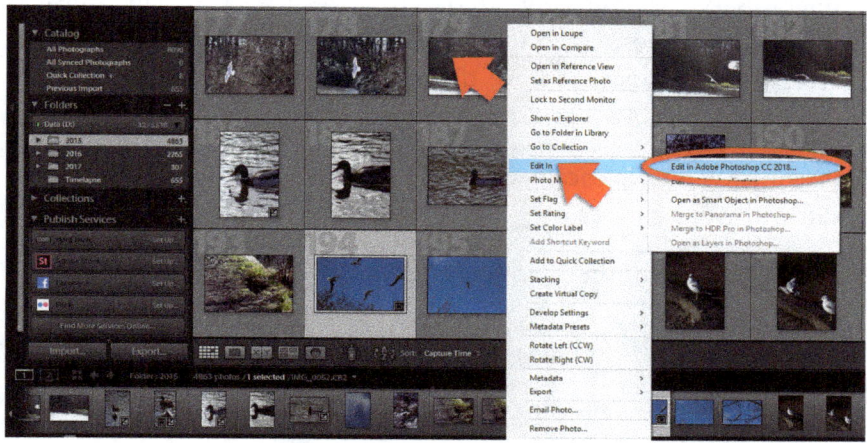

If you have adjusted the photograph in Lightroom you may be prompted with a few options. If not, the photo will open up in Photoshop.

If you want Lightroom to open the photo with the adjustments you have made, select 'edit a copy with Lightroom adjustments'. In not select 'edit original'.

Camera RAW

Camera RAW is your digital darkroom where you can adjust a photograph's exposure, brightness, adjust highlights or shadows, correct white balance, remove digital noise, as well as straighten up photographs, remove lens distortion and crop bits out.

Camera RAW automatically opens up when you open up a RAW image taken with your camera.

You can also find the Camera RAW filter on the filter menu in Photoshop.

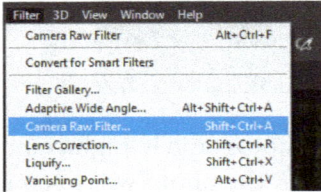

Lets take a look at the Camera RAW window.

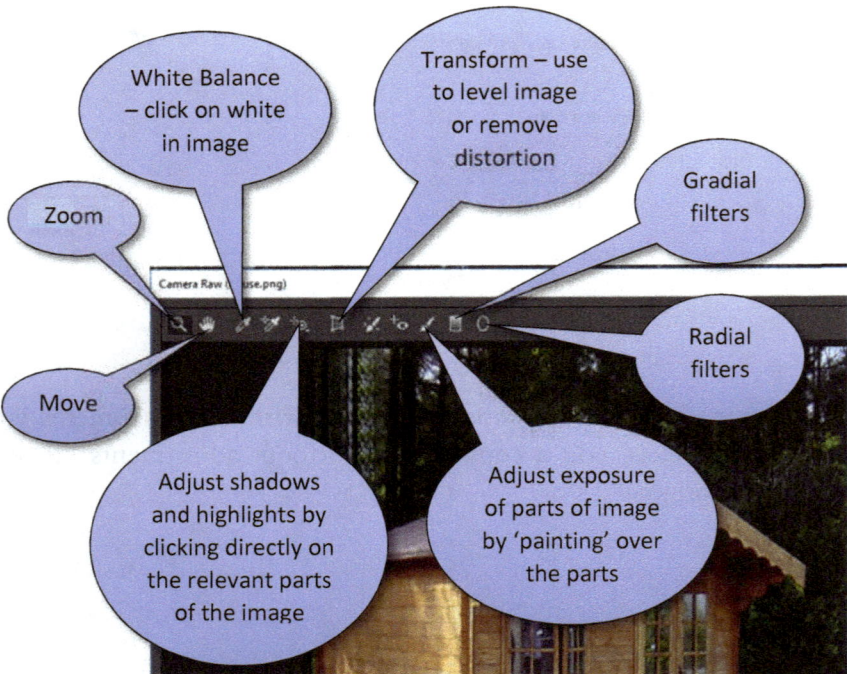

Reading a Histogram

The histogram shows the tonal range of a photograph - the range of brightness levels from pure black to pure white in the photo.

If all your peaks are squashed over to the left, the photograph is under exposed or too dark.

If all the peaks are squashed over to the right, your photo is over exposed or too bright.

This isn't always the case and depends on the photograph. For example, if a photograph has a lot of dark areas and shadows, then the histogram peaks will be more over to the left.

Lets take a closer look at the histogram. The histogram is split into five sections: Blacks, Shadows, Midtones, Highlights & Whites.

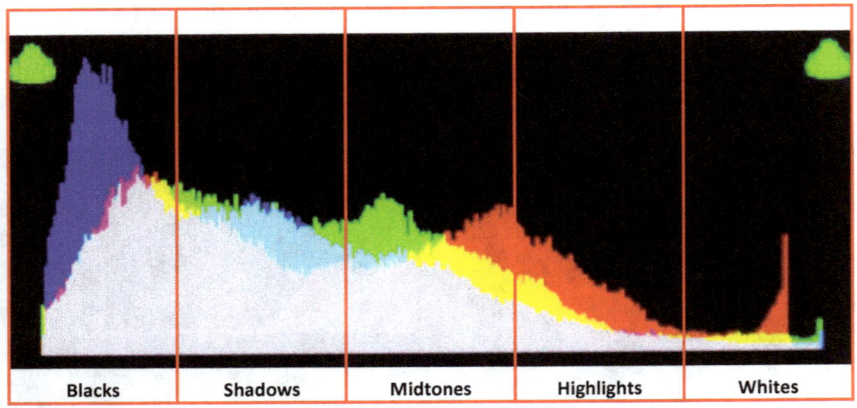

On a good histogram, most tones fall in the middle portion of the graph (shadows, midtones and highlights) with little or nothing at the extreme edges.

Also on the histogram you'll notice some colour. Photoshop histograms show the brightness levels for all the primary colours: red, green & blue channels (it also shows primary colours for print: yellow, cyan & magenta).

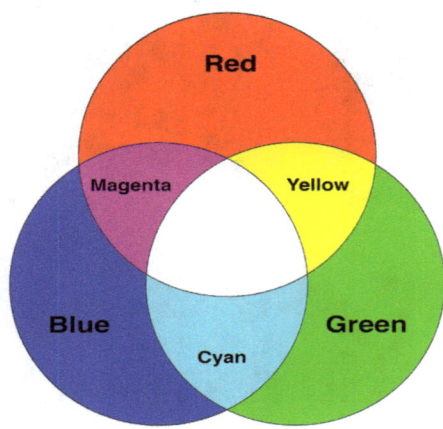

The light grey peak is the overall brightness. Don't worry too much about this now, for the scope of this exercise, concentrate on getting the peaks distributed across the five sections to achieve good exposure.

Adjusting a Photo

Open up **cameraraw.cr2** and have a go at adjusting the blacks, shadows, midtones, highlights and whites using the camera raw filter, until you get a nice evenly spread histogram. Keep an eye on the photograph to make sure looks evenly exposed. This photo was shot with a canon camera in raw format.

To adjust the photo, use the highlights, shadows, whites and blacks sliders to adjust the relevant levels on the histogram.

Use the exposure slider to adjust the overall brightness.

Keep in mind that the 'look' of the photograph will depend on the monitor you are using and whether it is correctly set up or calibrated. For example, if your brightness is turned up quite high on your monitor, your photo will look brighter than it actually is.

Leveling Photos & Removing Lens Distortion

When taking photographs, depending on what lens you use, there is always some kind of distortion. One of the most common issues seen when taking photographs of buildings and architecture, is the angle of walls.

Open **cathedral.jpg** and have a look.

Because the photographer has had to angle the camera upwards to get the whole tower in, the walls are all slanted inwards. Not a very professional looking photo.

You can use the camera raw filter to remove this distortion. Select the transform tool from the tool bar at the top of the camera raw window.

On the right hand side, under the histogram, you'll see some adjustment controls. First, try the auto adjustments along the top, sometimes these do a good enough job. I'm going to try auto first.

It did an ok job but didn't remove the distortion completely. To fine tune the adjustments, underneath you'll see some sliders. The vertical and horizontal controls work well with slanting walls. You will probably also need to enlarge the scale, using the scale slider, as the photo will warp a little bit when applying the corrections. Try them out, see what each slider does. Click OK on the bottom right when you're happy.

Looks a lot better right? You might lose some of the image, but it's a small price to pay for a better looking photograph.

Digital Images & Resolution

A digital image is an electronic representation of a photograph, image or artwork encoded in binary and stored on an electronic system such as a computer, tablet or smartphone.

Images Types

There are generally two types of images: bitmap images and vector images.

Bitmap Images

Also known as raster images, and uses thousands of pixels in varying colours and intensities to represent an image. Each pixel has a value, which specifies its colour and location.

When you work with bitmap images, you are editing pixels, rather than shapes. This allows for gradations of colour and creating a continuous tone appearance.

In the example above, because bitmap images contain a fixed number of pixels, they can lose detail or appear jagged edged when they are rescaled on the screen or printed at a higher resolution than they were created for. You can see above, in the yellow circle, what happens to the image as the size increases - you start to see the pixels.

Vector Images

A vector graphic, on the other hand, is made up of polygons defined by mathematical formulas in 2D or 3D space.

Because of this, you can move, resize or change the colour of the graphic without losing image quality.

This type of graphic is the best choice when you want a logo or bold graphic.

Resolution

Understanding how pixel data is measured and displayed will help you make decisions about your images both when scanning and working with the images in Photoshop.

Image Dimensions

How large an image displays on the computer screen is determined by the pixel dimensions of the image plus the size and setting of the monitor.

On a typical 15" monitor set to 800x600, an 800x600 image would fill the screen. This same image would fill the screen of a 19" inch monitor if it were also set to 800x600; each pixel on the 19" screen would be larger.

19" @ 800x600

15" @ 800x600

Likewise, if the 19" monitor were set to 1024x768, the image would appear much smaller.

19" @ 1024x768

Image Resolution

The number of pixels in an image determines the quality and detail of that image. Image resolution controls how much space these pixels are spread over when printed or displayed on screen.

A high resolution image contains more and therefore smaller pixels than an image with a low resolution. This means that a 1 inch by 1 inch image at 72 dpi would have 5184 pixels (72x72), whereas the same image at 300 dpi would have 90,000 pixels (300x300).

72 dpi   300 dpi

A higher resolution image produces more detail. However, increasing the resolution of an image only spreads the original pixel information over a larger number of pixels and will not improve image quality.

Most new monitors have a resolution of 96 dpi. No matter how high the resolution may be, we cannot see more than 96 pixels/inch in the displayed picture on a computer.

Printers vary widely, however your image should always be at least 300dpi if it is to be printed clearly.

Image Compression

High resolution RAW images can be very large without compression. so To save storage space and download times, images are compressed and saved as jpeg, png or tiff, depending on what they're being used for.

There are two basic types of compression, "lossy" and "lossless".

Lossy compression drops unnecessary pixel information from the original file. This is used in jpeg images. A side effect to lossy compression is a loss in quality the more the image is compressed.

Lossless compression retains all the pixel information. This is used in png images.

When working with images, it's best to work on your high resolution master images. These are usually your Photoshop files (PSD files).

The final images should be saved in the appropriate format (.png or .jpeg, etc.) in a folder called 'images' or 'exports' for the project. This insures that you will always have your high resolution originals available for future use or if you need to make changes.

You can export as a jpeg or png. To do this, go to the file menu and select 'export', from the slideout select 'export as'.

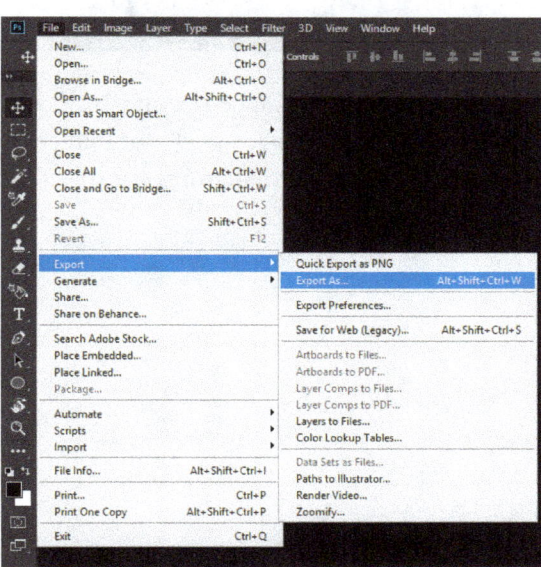

Appendix A: Digital Images & Resolution

From the dialog box you can select the image format on the top right, use either jpg or png.

For jpg, you can usually leave the quality at 100% for best results, however if you need to compress the image more, then reduce the quality. The lower this percentage the higher the compression.

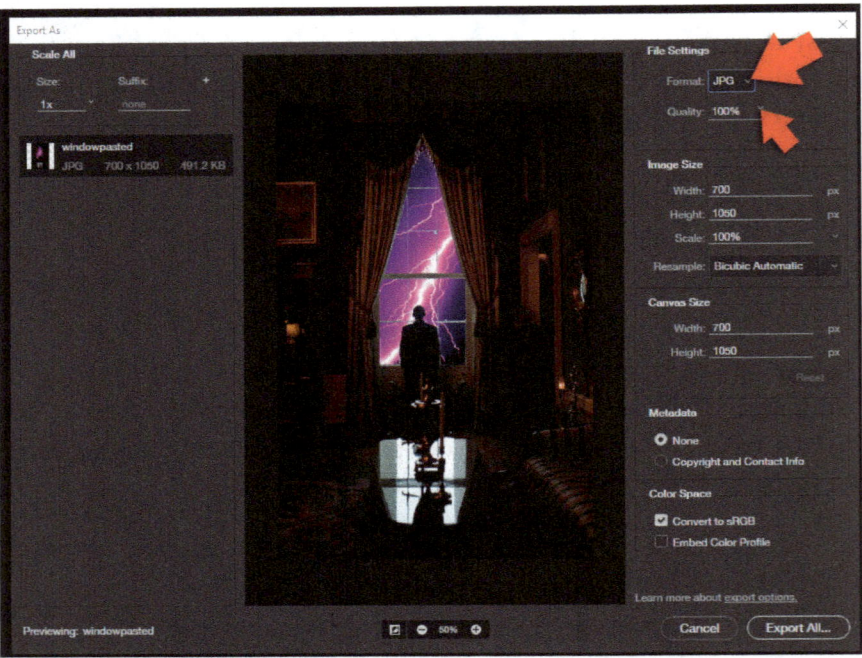

Underneath that, you can set the image size in pixels, or you can resize as a percentage size of the original size - 50% for half the size, 200% for double the size. This doesn't later the compression.

Common Image Formats

There are many different kinds of digital image file formats, each with their own capabilities and restrictions, here is a brief summary of the most common ones.

EPS "Encapsulated PostScript file" - used by programs such as PageMaker and Illustrator.

GIF A lossless image compression format, short for "Graphic Interchange Format" and is popular web icons, logos and buttons, but is limited to 8-bit (256 colours).

JPEG A lossy image compression format short for "Joint Photographic Experts Group" and is a popular format for saving photographs for use on the web or in printing.

PNG An image format using a lossless compression supporting 24-bit images (16.7 million colours) with transparency. This format is usually used on websites.

PSD Photoshop's native multiple layer image format. The format used to save all your multi-layer Photoshop projects.

RAW A raw format image is usually a photograph taken using a high end camera and is best used for high level photography where detail and the ability to adjust image tones and highlights are essential.

TIFF "Tagged Image File Format". These files tend to be either uncompressed or compressed using a lossless compression format and are commonly used in the printing and publishing industry.

i Index

Index

H

I

J

L

M

CPSIA information can be obtained
at www.ICGtesting.com
Printed in the USA
LVHW081617230819
628745LV00004B/36/P